Blue-Collar Buddha

Blue-Collar Buddha

Life-Changing Lessons Learned on the Journey
from Flight Attendant to Cancer Survivor
to Entrepreneurial Millionaire

PAUL A. STREITZ

ISBN 13: 978-0-615-53497-8

Printed in the United States of America

First Printing: 2012

16 15 14 13 12   5 4 3 2 1

Cover and interior design by James Monroe Design, LLC.

Streitz Media LLC.

StreitzMedia.com
BlueCollarBuddha.com

Available at Amazon.com

To my mother, Carol Louise Streitz,
who passed away on June 22, 2011 after a fourteen-year
struggle with cancer. By her courageous example, she taught
me how to be strong in the face of adversity and to live life
with dignity and compassion.

Contents

SECTION I:
CAREER HIGHLIGHTS AND LOWLIGHTS

SECTION II:
SCHOOL'S IN SESSION

SECTION III:
GETTING PERSONAL

SECTION IV:
FRIENDS AND LOVERS

Acknowledgments

I was the luckiest kid in the world because Jerome and Carol Streitz were my parents. Simply by the way they lived their lives, I learned how to honor others with love, respect, and forgiveness, and how to live a moral, ethical life.

My two brothers, Mike and Jerry, watched out for me when I was a kid like big brothers are supposed to do. They've always supported me, believed in me, and told me I could do anything and achieve anything I wanted to in life.

Without Phil Bolsta's help, my dream of writing this book would not have been possible. The way he took my rambling recollections and worked with me to turn them into well-crafted, entertaining stories was nothing short of magical. Thanks also to Erin O'Rourke for her editing skills.

I will always be grateful to my mentor, Tom Gegax, for seeing something special in me and showing me how to express it so I could teach and inspire others.

Thank you to the Brooklyn Center school system in Minnesota for being ahead of their time in the way they took care of me in fifth grade when my emotional well-being hung in the balance.

I wouldn't be half the man I am today if Paul Bruchard and Stuart Savage, my high school teaching heroes, hadn't taken me under their wings and made me feel special and important.

My deepest thanks to my Advanced Lighting Systems team for their trust in me and for trusting that our company would grow and evolve and become a major force in our industry. Time and time again, they rose to the challenge and made the impossible commonplace.

A huge shout-out to my longtime controller, Marlon Leischner. Marlon took a leap of faith by leaving a well-paying job to join Advanced Lighting as my first big hire. He was instrumental in our growth and indispensable in so many ways. He always had the company's best interests at heart and I'll forever be grateful to him for his faith in me.

Thank you to Janice O'Leary for helping me make it through my cancer scares and for inspiring me to become a better man.

Thank you to Krissy Smida, who stuck by me and believed in me during the early days of Advanced Lighting when I didn't even believe in myself.

Words cannot express my gratitude to Tim and Lovette Mieczkowski for being my dearest friends, encouraging me through all my ups and downs, and providing me with the material assistance I needed to start Advanced Lighting.

Special thanks to Russ Uhlenkamp for being one of my best friends on the planet. His insightful advice and well-reasoned opinions have kept me grounded and on the right track.

Foreword
By Tom Gegax

Had you met me back in 1989 when I was forty-two, you would've seen the facade of the classic American success story. I had the handsome family, the beautiful home. Every week I had time for church and shooting hoops with pals. I had a growing company and prominence in the community. I would've told you with an ear-to-ear grin and a firm handshake that life was good. Real good.

That's when life went all Humpty-Dumpty on me. Without warning, a triple trauma of divorce, cancer, and a company cash-flow crisis had me flattened on the pavement, surrounded by the shattered pieces of my life. My nerves were twitchy, downed power lines, forcing people to walk on eggshells around me as I tried to glue things back together. I lashed out at anyone who dared suggest I look in the mirror. I remember snapping at a friend not long after my divorce: "Show me anywhere in writing where it says it's healthy to feel my feelings!" One by one, my defenses were splintered by the wicked storm brewing inside me. I pummeled myself for six months: *You really screwed up. You hurt your family. You ruined your business. There's no way out of this one.* I was a dead man walking. Nothing in my life was going right, and it seemed like nothing would ever be right again.

I thought I had been Mr. Got-It-Covered. Instead, after many months of hard work, intense self-reflection, and even more intensive self-honesty, I realized how clueless I had been. The scary part was that I didn't have a clue that I didn't have a clue. Eventually, I returned to work and life a changed man. For the first time in my life, I was balanced, peaceful, and truly happy, both personally and professionally. In 2000, I sold Tires Plus, the retail tire store chain I had founded, for tens of millions of dollars. My journey back to wholeness, happiness, and abundance is chronicled in my two books: *Winning in the Game of Life: Self-Coaching Secrets for Success* and *The Big Book of Small Business: You Don't Have to Run Your Business by the Seat of Your Pants.*

Today, I find it enormously satisfying and rewarding to guide and mentor smart, savvy entrepreneurs who can benefit from the hard-earned wisdom I accumulated through my own struggles and successes. One of my prize pupils is Paul Streitz. Sensing he was at an important crossroads in life, Paul called me in 2004. He was forty-two, the same age I had been when the ground shifted under my feet. From our first meeting, I could tell there was something special about Paul. He was bright, funny, and an excellent businessman, but his seat-of-the-pants management style and lack of self-confidence were blocking him from greatness.

What especially impressed me about Paul was the ethical and transparent way that he ran his business and his life. His talent for both left-brain (logical and linear) and right-brain (intuitive and creative) thinking was rare among business leaders, as was his natural ability to be simultaneously extroverted and introspective. Perhaps most importantly, he genuinely cared for his employee family.

From the start, I was startled by how self-aware, honest, and non-defensive Paul was about his own flaws and insecurities. He was a good listener, a fast learner, and remarkably receptive and responsive to coaching. He wasn't satisfied with being really good at what he did; he wanted to be great. It was a pleasure to work with him, get to know him, and watch him blossom. Today, Paul is a trusted and valued business partner, and I look forward to many more years of mutual success and friendship.

The stories that Paul shares in this book are filled with uncommon wisdom and valuable pointers that can help anyone be happier and more successful while leading a balanced life. His experiences and insights are especially valuable for aspiring entrepreneurs, given that he founded and grew a vertically integrated company in a highly competitive industry. With visionary leadership, he guided his business through all the growth stages that a healthy, profitable enterprise demands, ultimately selling it for a handsome sum. In all aspects, Paul is a winner in the game of life, and I'm confident that he can help you become a big winner too.

Introduction

You can be happier than you are right now.

I don't care how messed up your life has been or still is. You can find a great relationship or improve the one you're in. You can have more friends. You can be more effective at work. You can make more money.

I never believed those things. Success and happiness were for smart people. Me? I was stupid. The closest I got to a report card full of A's was when I bumped into the class valedictorian in the hallway. English teachers cringed at my grammar and groaned over my spelling. I joined the Army Reserves as a junior because I thought that's what kids like me did. I figured I was destined to fix cars, watch sports, and drink beer for the next forty years.

Then something amazing happened at school: I stumbled into a program that encouraged and trained students to be business leaders and entrepreneurs. I discovered I was good at speaking and thinking on my feet and ended up winning third place at nationals. That summer in the army, I won the "Soldier of the Year" competition. I started thinking maybe I wasn't such a dummy after all. Instead of hating what was wrong with me, I began liking what was right with me.

I actually got a little cocky. Of course, that's when life just laughed at me and got serious about kicking my butt. After making it through two bouts of cancer in my early twenties, I got fired from my first two jobs in the lighting business and kept dating women who were great in their own right but completely wrong for me.

Figuring that successful people knew something I didn't, I attended a slew of personal-growth seminars that inspired me to work hard on improving my self-image. In time, I came to recognize that I had a lot to be proud of: I had a good heart, I had a good mind for the kind of work I did, and I did my best to always take the high road, just as my parents had taught me to do.

I was growing the successful lighting business I had started and had learned a ton of life and business lessons along the way, but I felt like I wasn't firing on all cylinders. I lacked a framework that tied everything together. Finally, at forty-two, I struck gold. I met a hugely successful businessman who became my mentor and one of my best friends. Tom, who I hired to be my business and life coach, showed me a whole new way of looking at the world and how to show up in it. He guided me to accept myself just as I was, flaws and all.

I quickly learned that when your inner world changes, your outer world can't help but follow suit. I became more confident, outgoing, and willing to take risks. Small successes gave way to big successes. Within two years, I sold my lighting company for several millions dollars.

Today, life is a nonstop adventure. I still can't spell to save my life, but I'm happier than I've ever been. I have a whole lot fewer insecurities, fears, and limiting beliefs about myself, and I'm psyched about all the cool stuff I'm involved in.

I'm especially excited about this book and how it can help you become happier and more successful and live a more peaceful and balanced life. I love sharing success secrets with others and hope that these stories uplift you, inspire you, and help you identify and conquer whatever fears are holding you back. Following each story are questions intended to spur self reflection, build self-awareness, and encourage self-improvement.

The fact that you picked up this book tells me there's something special about you. If you didn't feel the need to share your gifts with the world, if you didn't sense that there was greatness within you, you wouldn't feel compelled to pick up a book like this. I believe in people like you and I'm thrilled to play a role in helping you believe in yourself. Someone a lot more eloquent than me said it best:

> *Believe in your dreams and they may come true;*
> *believe in yourself and they will come true.*

Section I

CAREER HIGHLIGHTS AND LOWLIGHTS

It's appropriate that I was a flight attendant because I started out in the business world flying by the seat of my pants. No regrets though; I learned more from my setbacks than I did from my successes.

FLYING HIGH

If not for a pretty woman in a car lot, I never would have gotten into the lighting business. She and her husband were buying a new car from me at the dealership where I worked. He seemed like a nice guy but he was pretty average looking. I thought, *What's he doing with a girl like her?* When I had a moment alone with him, I said, "Dude, how'd you meet such a smoking hot girl?" He laughed and said that she was a flight attendant and he managed the airport parking area. He asked her out and they hit it off.

When she joined us a minute later, I told her it was so cool that she worked for an airline. I said, "I've always wanted to be a flight attendant; I could fly all over the world and just think of all the girls I could meet!" They both laughed and I added that flying would be perfect for me; I could learn about business and have enough free time to figure out what I wanted to do with my life.

I was twenty-three and the only reason I was selling cars was because all my relatives were in the car business. I was pretty good at it but didn't like it much. I had always wanted to be an entrepreneur but didn't have any idea how to get started. I hadn't gone to college, didn't have any marketable skills, and my dad was a union leader who thought I should get a real job.

A couple days later, the couple came back to close the deal for their car. She handed me a newspaper ad from American Airlines and said, "We're not going to sign the papers for the car until you call these guys up and ask for an interview to be a flight attendant." So I said I would. She added, "Tell them you speak another language; it will help you get an interview."

Two weeks after I sent an application to American Airlines, I got a phone call asking me to fly down to Dallas for an interview. I was both excited and nervous; excited because it sounded like a dream job, and nervous because I had mentioned I was learning French but I didn't know a croissant from a coup de grace. I raced to the want ads, found a French teacher, and spent twelve hours cramming.

They flew me down there and bam, I landed the job! The recruiter told me they got fifty thousand applicants a month and were only hiring three thousand people, but I came out on top because I was "so real and so fun to be around." I thought that was cool. I later found out that even though the airline was flooded with applicants, they continued to advertise in the Midwest because of the honesty and work ethic of the people there. Speaking of which, they never did ask me to speak French!

I moved to Dallas, and just like that, I was serving coffee to first-class passengers at thirty thousand feet. The other flight attendants hated working first class; they saw nothing but pompous, needy people. I thought it was awesome because I was all gung ho to be an entrepreneur and here was a captive audience that knew everything I wanted to know. I worked those aisles like crazy. I'd ask passengers, "So tell me, why are you sitting here instead of in coach? What did you do right?" Guess what? Most people love to talk about how they became successful. I heard so many terrific stories and got so many great ideas. I ate it all up and kept coming back for more. I felt like I was getting paid to go to college.

During a layover in Reno, I was checking out a casino and noticed that one of the restaurants was roped off and shut down. I saw guys inside installing shooting stars in black ceiling tiles and thought, *Wow, that is so cool.* One of the guys was on a ladder near me so I tugged on his shorts and said, "Hey, what are you doing?" He said "We're making a fiber optic starfield ceiling." I asked him who he worked for and he told me about FiberNev, the small family company that his parents ran as a hobby.

I loved what he was doing and wanted to be a part of it so I blurted out, "Hey, can I work for you?" He told me his name was Danny and that I should call his dad, George, so I did. George told me that the fiber optic industry, at least with regard to the applications his company was offering, was still in its early stages and there was lots of opportunity. He appreciated my enthusiasm but told me he didn't have a job for me. I said, "Well, how about if I go out selling for you and you only pay me if I bring in new business?" He was open to that, so we negotiated a 15 percent commission.

Whenever I had a day off from flying, I'd call on as many video rental stores, movie theaters, and mom-and-pop shops as I could. If there was an OPEN sign on the door, I said, "Hey, you want to buy an OPEN sign that twinkles and glitters and changes colors?" I had expected big commissions, but after eight months I had yet to make my first sale.

No mater how much I tried to keep my spirits up, I felt like I was sinking deeper into failure and self-loathing. I was seriously bummed during a flight back to the Dallas hub in June 1989 until I started talking to a passenger named Manny. He said he was a store-planning architect for Chuck E. Cheese's so I told him about fiber optics and that I was sure that kids would love it at their venues. I also confessed that I was a complete bust and hadn't made one sale. He said, "I'll tell you why, Paul. Stores that are already open have spent all their floor plan money and all they care about is selling their product. You need to get to new stores that are in the planning stages so they can build your signs into their budget." Manny's encouraging words started pumping air into my deflated dreams. I got even more fired up when he said, "Come by my office in Irving soon. I'll take a look at your stuff." How perfect was that? Irving, Texas was where I lived! By the time we touched down, I wanted to tear the door off the hinges and hit the ground running.

A week later, I met Manny at his office, showed him some samples and we hit on the idea of embedding fiber optics in a stage curtain so the Chuck E. Cheese character would be backed by twinkling stars. I flew back to FiberNev in Reno, got some demos made, flew back to Texas and presented them to Manny in July. He thought they were great but was a bit concerned about the illuminator that lit up the fiber; it was reliable but it didn't look very sturdy. He said, "If this thing lasts for six months, I'll call you in six months and one day and we'll order fiber optic curtains for all 1,100 stores." I was pumped up but when I called George, he said, "It sounds great, Paul, but it's basically a brush-off."

I could tell Manny was a man of his word but four months after our conversation, my life got put on hold when I was diagnosed with testicular cancer (see the "Conquering Cancer" chapter for the full story). That knocked me out of action for a bit but, I finished a thirty-one-day radiation treatment just in time to call Manny and say, "Hi, Manny, it's six months and one day today." He said, "That's right, and your lights are still working. I want you to come in."

Because of the cancer surgery and treatment, I hadn't had a chance to get a prototype made. I was on my ten-week sick leave from the airline but could still fly free as needed, so I flew out to FiberNev and got to work. George and I tried a bunch of configurations and finally nailed it. I couldn't wait to fly back and show Manny the prototype. Sure enough, he loved it. The next day, I was in my underwear at home when I heard the fax machine ring in the guest bedroom. I went to investigate and there was a purchase order for a few hundred thousand dollars, more than three times the net worth of FiberNev. I wish I had video of that moment because I was dancing around in my underwear like Tom Cruise in "Risky Business." Yeah, baby!

Flying High
Your Life, Your Thoughts

- What were some of the unexpected twists and turns that led you into your current career?

- What are some of the best business or life lessons you learned from either talking to or reading about successful people?

- What opportunities have you created for yourself through your positive energy and creative thinking?

- Taking a few minutes to brainstorm right now, what new professional, social, or life opportunities can you envision creating for yourself in the next six months?

- What are three ways you can think of to meet new people whom you can build mutually beneficial relationships with?

- Thinking back on some of your biggest wins in business or in life, what if anything did you do back then that you're not doing today?

PROMISES, PROMISES

With Chuck E. Cheese signing a multiyear contract for fiber optic curtains, FiberNev became a three-quarter of a million dollar company overnight. It was awesome. I kept raking in commissions and, of course, George, the owner, loved me. I was the golden boy with the Midas touch.

Five months after the Chuck E. Cheese deal, George told me that Euro Disney, the new theme park just outside of Paris (now called Disneyland Paris) was under construction and using a ton of fiber optics. He was upset that we couldn't get any of the business because France passed a law that every company working on Euro Disney had to be a French company. "We're out of it," George said. "There's nothing we can do." I said, "Wait a minute. You're telling me that everything that Disney needs, there's a French company that can supply it? Disney does tons of amazing special effects, there's no possible way that everything can be built by French companies." George just shrugged and said, "That's the law." I said, "Let me investigate this."

I've never understood how people can throw their hands up in the air at the first sign of a road-block. Since I could fly free internationally, I hopped on a plane, landed in France, and started visiting specialty lighting companies. Right away, I ran into a super-rich family from Lebanon that owned a prestigious company. I met them at their office and said, "You're not in the fiber optic business, so let's do a joint venture. We'll share our skill, which will allow you to get contracts from Euro Disney and we'll both share in the profits." They thought it was a fantastic idea.

I went back and told George, "Okay, here's the deal. I've got a company willing to sign a joint venture agreement with us. And just so you know, that's what all the American companies are doing that do work for Disney." We signed an agreement with the French lighting company and set up George's son, Danny, in an apartment in France. I flew back and forth, and we did millions of dollars in business with Euro Disney. And it was all because I told myself, "There's got to be a way to make this happen."

Before long, we were doing so much business, including work from Disneyland in the U.S., that we opened an office and factory in Dallas for me to run. Sometimes I had to stop and remind myself how far I had come in just a couple of years. Here I had been a deadbeat car salesman who wanted to be an entrepreneur but didn't have a clue where to begin. I took the advice of a pretty customer, ended up tugging on some guy's pants, built up his family's company, and made a truckload of money. It all seemed like a dream. Funny thing about dreams; they can all too easily turn into nightmares.

I should have suspected something was up when my commissions started mounting and I wasn't getting paid. Being young and dumb, I told George, "Hey, I know you'll pay me, don't worry about it." One day, George came to me and said, "We're going to make you part owner of the company; we'll give you 10 percent." I was thrilled. I was on my way!

I ramped up my efforts to find new leads and bring in new sales. I went to three trade shows back to back to back and racked up all the expenses on my personal credit cards: travel, hotel, food, entertainment, booth space, and trade show services. When I submitted my expense report for $40,000 of business-related expenses, George very casually said, "Paul, you're part owner now, we can't afford to pay you all this money. You need to do what's best for the company. When the going's great we make a lot of money, but when things slow down we all have to take a hit." Whoa. The blinders fell off and I realized I was only working for my 10 percent stake in the company. I felt like the pit of my stomach had dropped to the floor. Not only weren't they going to reimburse me for my expenses, I could forget about the 30 grand in commissions I had coming to me too.

Here I had single-handedly built up FiberNev into an industry powerhouse and George slipped me the green weenie like I was a guy off the street. I told him, "Look, you've got to pay me this money. You left me with forty grand worth of expenses on my credit cards." He just said, "Sorry, we can't do that. Business has been bad. Just go out and get more sales." I put up a fight and things got ugly real quick. Turns out George had been spending lavishly on luxury cars and boats and traveling around the world. He had totally mismanaged the company's funds and was robbing Peter to pay Paul. Well, guess what? I was Paul and they robbed me blind as the money petered out.

I knew I had to leave the company. I had an attorney write George a letter demanding that he pay me, but George's response was, "Sorry, we don't have any money." I could have fought it but it would have cost me money I didn't have and I would have ended up with nothing anyway because a year after I left, FiberNev was out of business.

Even though I was saddled with debt, I decided the best thing to do was just walk away and keep moving, painful as it was. I rebounded quickly, landing a job with TexGlow, a lighting company in Dallas owned by two brothers named Eric and Alex Goodman. The Goodmans recognized that fiber optic lighting was the next big thing and wanted in on the action. They made fiber optic cable but wanted to start manufacturing products that used the cable instead of just being a cable provider. After helping them get set up in the business, I spent two years building up the division.

One day I walked into work and the owner said, "We've got to talk to you." I cheerfully said, 'Sure, what's up?" He said, "You're giving away our trade secrets." I said, "What? How am I doing that?" He told me that when I brought a furniture maker into the warehouse, someone overheard me telling him how to put fiber optics in his products, like under a bed to make it glow. I said, "That's not how it went. He's ordering $5,000 worth of illuminators and fiber, which we sell all the time in raw form, because he has to install the cable himself. His furniture pieces are very custom and expensive, and he can't ship them here and trust that we wouldn't screw up the lacquer or whatever. All I did was tell him what size drill bit he'd need to mount his cable, which we tell other customers all the time over the phone; he just happens to be local." They said, "We don't think that's right." I said, "I'm sorry you don't think it's right but we do it all the time." They said, "Well, we're going to have to let you go."

Excuse me? That just didn't make sense. Just like at FiberNev, I built that division up from nothing, made the owners a ton of money, and then they plugged me in the back and dumped me in the river. I was steamed. It was the second time I was taken advantage of. Later, I found out that they wanted to get rid of me because they were selling the company and they had handshake-promised me 25 percent of the division that built the fiber optic products. Sure enough, six months after I was gone, they sold the company. Firing me saved them a whole bunch of money.

For the next nine months or so I felt sorry for myself and didn't do much other than my flight attendant shifts. I thought, *Screw this, I'm done. Everybody's ripping me off.* I felt like a victim, like I was never going to recover, like I had blown my only chances to make it. Then I had an epiphany. I realized, *Wait a minute, these guys are seventy years old. I'm less than half their age. They're at the end and I've got all sorts of time to show these guys up.*

Looking back, getting ripped off at both FiberNev and TexGlow were the best things that could have happened because I learned such valuable lessons. The first lesson was to get everything in writing. My 10 percent ownership in FiberNev and 25 percent in TexGlow's fiber optics division were worthless without a signed contract. That was a tough lesson to learn. I was just a good old Midwestern boy who thought people would stand by their promises.

The second lesson was, if an offer looks too good to be true, look deeper for the motivation behind it. When FiberNev offered me 10 percent of the company, I thought it was because they valued me and were afraid of losing me. In reality, they were taking advantage of my naïveté and manipulating me into funneling more money into the company for the owner to spend on his luxury toys.

After both companies hammered me so badly, I could have easily justified declaring bankruptcy. But I was determined not to as a matter of principle. Now, I'm not saying I wouldn't file bankruptcy in extreme circumstances or diss anybody who does, but I knew I'd feel better about myself if I cleaned up the mess I was in and got back on my feet the hard way. I had about 25 grand in the bank so that covered more than half my debt. I raised more cash by selling my Rolex and getting a cheaper car. Even though I was still mired in a pity party, I picked up every extra flight I could and managed to be cheerful with the passengers. I also negotiated with the credit card companies, which dinged my credit report a bit, but that enabled me to pay everything off within a year. Sending in that last payment felt phenomenal, knowing how hard I had worked to make that happen.

I see now that those lessons could have been a lot more expensive than they were. Now that I think about it, the debt I racked up and the money I should have been paid all added up to what a college tuition would have cost me. And boy, did I get an education!

Promises, Promises
Your Life, Your Thoughts

- If you don't have a "There's always a way to get things done" attitude, how can you challenge yourself to think more creatively and positively?

- What lessons did you learn from the dumb mistakes you've made?

- In your professional interactions, how can you strike a better balance between trust and caution?

- What steps can you take to protect yourself in your financial agreements with others?

- What, if anything, has stopped you from keeping your promises and what can you do to fix that?

THE MEXICAN CARTEL

TexGlow had hired me to ramp up their visibility and rope in new accounts. So six months in, I convinced the Goodmans to pony up for a booth at the IAAPA (International Association of Amusement Parks and Attractions) Expo. Since we were in the business of creating magic with lights, I figured a trade show was a great opportunity for networking and generating leads.

The first morning of the show, I was all psyched to do some deals and impress my bosses but I was also nervous. I had never done a trade show before and was just feeling my way around. Mid-morning, up walks a sharp-looking guy with an entourage. He said his name was Manuel, made a little conversation and said our lights and signs were just what he needed. I said, "Great! That's why we're here." He said, "I need you to come out to my facility in Mexico City and tell me what I need." Mexico sounded like an awesome place to visit but since my bosses were standing right there I said, "I'm sure you understand that we can't just jump on an airplane on the chance that we might get some business from you." He said, "No problem. Tomorrow morning I'll have an airline ticket for you." He wanted me to come see him the Tuesday after the show. One of his associates grabbed my card and they left. The Goodmans and I looked at each other and laughed. We thought he was just playing us. The rest of the day was uneventful. I made a few contacts and got a few business cards but I was still worried I had wasted my bosses' money.

Early the next morning, a guy shows up and identifies himself as Alberto, Manuel's brother. He was a younger guy, very polished and professional. I was impressed. He had the look of a very successful man, exactly what I wanted to be. He held out his hand and said, "Here's your ticket." The ticket was Dallas to Mexico City, full-fare, first class. After Alberto left, I showed the Goodmans the ticket and said, "These guys are serious. No way some guy's going to spend $2,800 flying me down there for nothing. He's sending a message: 'I mean business: I'm going to buy. Don't even question that.'"

The rest of the day flew by. The more I thought about flying down to Mexico City, the more excited and anxious I got. I wanted everything to go perfectly but I was so young and inexperienced that I didn't have a clue about what to expect.

Two days after the show ended, I was on a flight to Mexico. The first thing I saw when we landed was guys with machine guns waiting in the passenger walkway between the terminal and the jet. I felt like I was on a different planet. As I walked toward the terminal entrance, someone said, "You're Paul Streitz. Come with me." I followed him as he walked me right through customs. The whole experience was so surreal that I didn't know what to think. My adrenaline was pumping and I was a little afraid for my safety but I also felt important. I thought, *Man, I've arrived in the big world of business. I'm a player now. I'm in, I'm good.*

Things were moving pretty fast. A couple of big dudes loaded up my luggage into a black SUV, one of six identical vehicles with blacked-out windows. It reminded me of a presidential entourage. I got in one of the SUVs with Manuel; his brother Alberto was in another vehicle because they didn't want to ride together. Manuel started telling me how important a businessman he was, about how you need to make things happen and jump on opportunities. I could tell he liked me; he was giving off a big brother vibe. I soaked it all up, too naïve to notice the red flags popping up left and right.

We pulled up in front of a two-level building in Mexico City and went inside. The lower level was a huge video game arcade, about 120 feet wide by 300 feet long; the second level was half that size with a balcony overlooking the first floor. All the games were set up and ready to go but they all had plastic protective covering.

Manuel gestured around the room and said he wanted to load the place up with fiber optic effects and signage. He said, "Give me ideas." When I asked if he had a budget, he acted like I had insulted him. He said, "Do I look like a man with a budget? Don't tell me about a budget. Tell me what I need."

I managed to keep my nerves in check and pointed out a back wall that looked to be 20 feet tall by 20 feet wide. I said, "Well, the first thing you need to do is fill this back wall with lights." He said, "Done!" I said, "Well, what do you want?" He said, "You figure it out." I took a picture of the wall and kept moving.

I glanced around and said, "Think about this: At the top of every slot machine in Vegas, there's some sort of signage or glittery display that attracts you to that bank of machines. We could do that to every single one of your banks of games. We could even market specific machines with top signs and end cap signs. You might even be able to get the manufacturers of the games to help you with the costs." He shot me a look. "That's not important," he said. "Just tell me what I need."

Manuel was not a guy to mess with. He had a hair-trigger temper. Every time a guy came up to us and interrupted our conversation, he'd blow up. He was in the guy's face, screaming, spit flying everywhere. But a minute later, he was mellow again. This was a guy who wanted people to fear him.

While I was taking pictures of the banks of machines, I looked up and saw that Manuel had disappeared and that his brother had taken his place. Alberto asked me how much everything would cost. I shrugged and said, "Well, every little strand of fiber is one-sixteenth of an inch; depending on what we do I could use millions of feet of fiber or not. I just don't know yet." He said, "Well, he's going to want a price by the time you leave." I fought off a wave of panic and said, "Well, all right. I'll do what I can."

Alberto then motioned me upstairs to what looked like a very large control room. There was nothing in there but armed security guards, computers, and machines counting money. Being a simple-minded Midwestern boy, I'm saying to myself, *I don't get it. They're not even open. Where's the money coming from?*

Two minutes later, we were back in the fleet of SUVs. On the way back to my hotel, Alberto told me they'd pick me up for dinner. Back in my room, I called my bosses and said, "This guy wants me to give him a price tonight. How am I supposed to do that for such a huge order? He told me that money's no object so I guess I'll just give him a high number." The Goodmans were excited but cautious. They said, "Okay, Paul, but don't spoil it by getting greedy." I said, "I'm not greedy. I just want to give this guy what he wants."

Only a couple of vehicles showed up to take me to dinner but the other four SUVs were waiting for us down the road, and merged in when we drove by. We pulled up to a place that was clearly a best-in-Mexico-City kind of restaurant. As soon as we walked in, the maître d' and owner came over and hugged everyone like they were old pals. The restaurant had been a quarter full when we got there but within minutes the other customers had all left, many of them with food and wine still on the table. Nobody asked them to leave, they just did. I looked around at the empty room, bewildered.

The twelve of us sat down at a long table with a beautiful spread. Outside, a few guys stood in the front of the restaurant with machine guns, but I just told myself, *Well, he's an important man and I don't know what kinds of things go on in Mexico City.* Every step of the way, I was trying to justify to myself what was going on because I couldn't figure out all the strange behavior.

Right at the start of our meal, out came a super-expensive bottle of red wine called Rothschild, and I'm thinking, *Crap, I've never had wine before. This guy doesn't take no for an answer, so I'll just have to grin and bear it.* They poured me a glass, I took a few sips and thought, *Wow, this is fantastic!* It took me years to realize that I was introduced to wine with one of the best brands money can buy.

In the middle of dinner, Manuel looked at me and said, "So how much is everything going to cost? Tell me now." I said, "I can only give you an estimate because I don't want to tell you too high a price and take advantage of your generosity." He said, "Just give me a number." I said, "Okay, it's going to be three-quarters of a million dollars." He said, "No problem. You go back, you send me designs, you give me the bank information, and I'll wire the money."

After dinner, Manuel took off in one of the SUVs and Alberto and I rode back to my hotel. The ride was long enough for Alberto and me to have a nice talk. He wasn't much older than me but he sure had a lavish lifestyle. He told me about a home his family owned in Acapulco. When he described it and said it had once been Sylvester Stallone's home, I knew exactly what house he was talking about because I had seen it during one of my layovers as a flight attendant. "I know that house," I told him. "It's incredible. A big white house right on the cliffs." To a kid like me, it was paradise. Alberto smiled and said, "You can use the house any time you want, Paul. You're part of our family now." *Wow, how cool is that?* I thought. *I've really arrived!*

I flew back home the next morning. When I told my bosses everything that happened, they said, "I don't know, Paul. I think you just got taken for a ride." I said, "Why would someone fly me in first class, take me out to dinner, and treat me that well if he was full of crap? I think the guy's good for it."

I got busy, produced some designs on storyboards, and FedExed them to Manuel just a few days after I got back from Mexico. The next day there was $350,000 in our bank account. We were blown away. That deal drilled into me that I should never judge whether someone was a real buyer or not. Manuel was an over-the-top kind of guy but he followed through on everything he promised.

Manuel bought tickets for Jim, one of our engineers, and me to fly back down to Mexico City to take exact measurements. When we arrived at the airport, Alberto accompanied us to the arcade. I remember Jim looking at me as we were working and saying, "Something just doesn't seem right here, Paul. Do you get the same vibe?" I said, "Yep, I don't get it. But hey, we've got his money already so let's do what we need to do and get out of here." We finished up, Alberto signed off on everything, and we flew back home.

Four weeks later, we had all the product ready for delivery. I called Manuel, told him everything was done and that we needed the rest of the payment. He said, "No problem. I'll send my airplane up and we'll pick it up next week." That surprised us a little bit but it was doable because TexGlow was located in an old airplane hanger at Dallas' Addison Airport. We had converted the facility into a factory but you could still literally park an airplane right behind our building.

A few days later, Alberto called and said he and the pilot were taking off and they'd be there in two and a half hours. That got us scrambling. The plan was for Alberto to arrive and inspect the equipment. Once he signed off on the order, it would take a few hours to pack the equipment up and load it on the plane. During that time, the bank wire could be authorized and sent.

When Alberto arrived—on a jet, no less—we quickly learned that he had a different plan. He inspected the product, handed me a suitcase and said, "Here's the money." Whoa. Four hundred grand in cash. I looked at my bosses and said, "You deal with this." They took the cash and off went the equipment. Three weeks later, Alberto called me. "We want to install the equipment," he said. "Can you fly somebody down to help us? But you have to be with them, Paul, because we trust you."

Off I went again to Mexico. The installation went smoothly and I was back home the next day, feeling like a hero. The whole deal had gone off perfectly. I made a lot of money, the company made a lot of money and I now had the confidence to go after bigger deals.

But that wasn't the end of my Mexico adventure. Fast-forward a year. During a layover in Mexico City, I told one of the crew members, "Hey, listen. I did a huge job down here not far from where we're staying. Let's go check it out." We hopped in a taxi, drove to the arcade, and peeked in the windows. All of the machines were still covered with plastic and none of our signs were lit up. It was late afternoon, prime time for kids to be there playing. There was a lot of traffic going in and out, but trust me, none of them were kids.

Fast-forward another year. I was back in Mexico City. The arcade still was not open. A couple of months later, I ran into Alberto at one of the finest hotels in Dallas, where I was meeting a friend for lunch. Alberto had just had a manicure and massage and was relaxing in a robe by the pool, wearing a big Rolex and drinking a scotch. When I walked over, he said, "Hey, Paul, how's it going?" I said, "Great, Alberto. How's the product working out for you?" He said, "Just great; kids love it." I told him I was happy to hear that and that was the last I saw of him.

Eventually, it dawned on me that Manuel and Alberto were laundering money. I had wondered why they were messing around with a video game arcade, but then I realized that they needed to have a cash-generating business so they could give the authorities a legitimate reason why they had so much cash on hand.

I still feel a little guilty about conveniently ignoring all the little signs that should have told me something criminal was going on. I had relished making money off the project but I see now that it was probably at the expense of the suffering of a lot of people. If Internet search engines had been around, I could have easily checked the guy out before committing to anything. I'd like to think that I would have steered clear of deals like that had I known what was going on, but I can't be sure. I was young and easily impressed by people who looked and acted like big shots.

I wish I would have listened to my gut feeling, but back then I didn't put much stock in intuition. If something didn't feel right, I brushed any misgivings aside and figured out some way to rationalize going forward with what I wanted to do. As I got older and more self-aware, I realized that my gut feeling is a surefire way to tell right from wrong. If Manuel approached me today for the first time, I'd pay attention to the warning signs. I'd still act professional; I'd just make it difficult enough to do business with me that he'd walk away from the deal. No matter how tempting a deal may be, a clear conscience beats a big payday every time.

The Mexican Cartel
Your Life, Your Thoughts

- How comfortable are you with stepping outside your comfort zone and challenging yourself to learn new and better ways to do your job?

- In what ways would taking more risks potentially help or hurt your professional and personal lives?

- When red flags pop up in your dealings with people, what are you thinking and how do you respond?

- What types of personalities do you most have trouble dealing with?

- What are three things you could do that might help you cope better with demanding people or intimidating situations?

- In what kind of situations can you see yourself relaxing your integrity when it's convenient to do so?

- In those times when you ignored your gut feeling and plowed straight ahead, in what ways was your intuitive concern justified?

BLOOD IS THICKER
THAN BUSINESS

My brother Jerry was working with me at TexGlow when his wife insisted on moving back to Minnesota. So Jerry quit and they drove a thousand miles from Dallas back to Sauk Centre. Literally the moment after Jerry unloaded the car, his wife told him, "I want a divorce."

Six months later, in the fall of 1992, TexGlow fired me. After getting played for a sucker by two companies, I figured the best way to protect myself from unethical bosses was to start my own company and be my own boss. But for nine months, I was too busy feeling sorry for myself to even think about jumping into anything new. In the meantime, I at least had put my head down, worked hard, and paid off my debt.

Shortly after TexGlow eighty-sixed me, Jerry had started a small-scale fiber optic lighting company in Sauk Centre. He ran it out of the basement of a building owned by his best friend, chiropractor Tim Mieczkowski. Tim was a great guy and was happy to help out. I flew back from Dallas a few times to help Jerry get set up, but I didn't want any part of the company myself.

Nearly a year after starting his business, Jerry called me. He wanted to grow the company and asked me to join him. But I knew my brother. I said, "Jerry, this isn't a good fit. If I'm going to run a company, I want to become big, like *big* big, like making the *Inc.* magazine list big. You're a gypsy kind of guy; if you have ten bucks in your pocket, life is great." He protested, insisting that he had matured and was ready to get down to business and make a better life for his two kids. He sounded so sincere that I started entertaining the idea. Finally, I told him, "Listen, partnerships are like a marriage. We're brothers and that's never changing. But we have to have shared goals and expectations before we do this. You're not incorporated, you're not an LLC, you're just cashing checks and calling yourself Advanced Lighting. We need to formalize the business and our agreements with each other." That's a lesson I had learned the hard way after getting worked over by FiberNev and TexGlow.

Jerry said he was on board so we had a cousin of ours who was an attorney draw up our corporate documents. We incorporated as Advanced Lighting Systems, Inc. because Tim's business was called Advanced Chiropractic. His receptionist could then answer the phone, "Advanced," and direct callers to either one of us. As a thank you to Tim, who was letting us use his space and his phones at no cost, we wrote him in as 10 percent owner of the company. We wanted to do something special to mark the launch of the new-and-improved Advanced Lighting, so Tim, Jerry, and I went out on Tim's pontoon and signed our corporate documents in the middle of Sauk Lake.

A year after I teamed up with Jerry, we had grown enough to get our own space. We wanted to repay Tim for his kindness but he just waved it off. He said, "You don't owe me anything. I'm just happy to see you guys succeed." When I told Tim we had to legally record a transaction that showed us buying back his shares, he shrugged and said, "How about a dollar?" Jerry and I talked about it and decided to surprise Tim by giving him $2,500. Tim not only helped us get our business up and running, his generosity and selflessness were a welcome breath of fresh air when I needed it most.

Jerry and I made an awesome team. He ran the shop and oversaw production while I was in charge of the office and sales. I was proud to work the trade shows with him and it felt great to know that I was helping him become a success. I was still living in Dallas and working as a flight attendant but I'd be in the office in Sauk Centre at least two days a week. Jerry had rebounded well from his divorce and was working hard and applying himself like I had always hoped he would.

Early in 1996, Jerry met a woman named Leslie. When he introduced us, I could tell she was quick-witted and intelligent, but my gut feeling was that she was a little rough around the edges. Jerry was clearly smitten so I just shrugged and hoped for the best. It didn't take long for those hopes to get dashed.

The more seriously Jerry became involved with Leslie, the more strained my relationship with him became. One day, when Jerry was out of town and I was leaving to go back to Dallas, I asked Dora, our office manager, to cut me a thousand-dollar check because I was short on cash. I told her that I would let Jerry know about it. I didn't want Jerry to find out through Dora because we had an agreement that if one of us took money, we'd immediately tell the other about it. In those pre-cell phone days, however, there was no way for me to get hold of Jerry until he got back in town two days later. Before I could reach him, he found out about the check and accused me of stealing a thousand dollars. Exasperated, I said "Jerry, if I was stealing a thousand dollars, do you really think I'd have a check written directly to me? If I wanted to hide it, I would have taken it out in cash." I told Jerry to ask Dora what happened and she backed me up 100 percent. Even so, my explanation didn't satisfy him.

Advanced Lighting was doing well enough in May of 1997 that I felt I was needed there full time. When I told Sean, my supervisor at American Airlines, that I was quitting, he told me to come back in a week. Puzzled, I asked him why. He said, "Just trust me, come back in a week." A week later, I went back and told him, "I want to quit. Here's my resignation letter." He said, "Nope, I can't accept that. But you qualify for early retirement. I'll accept that." It turns out he knew that a new rule in our contract was about to go into effect that would make early retirement available to employees whose combined age and number of years served reached a certain threshold. My timing was perfect; I barely qualified for a cash payout and lifetime passes for my family and me. Thanks, Sean. Good looking out!

I was excited to move to Sauk Centre and build something great with my brother, but Leslie, who had recently joined Advanced Lighting, had other ideas. She considered herself a smart businesswoman and acted professionally enough, but I got a weird competitive vibe from her. Sure enough, Jerry told me much later that Leslie had been badgering him to break off and form a lighting company of their own. "What do you need your brother for?" she'd tell him. "I'm better than he is. We can do everything ourselves." Jerry, blinded by love, bought what she was selling.

I was concerned about the growing rift in my relationship with my brother, but not overly so. I figured that once I was on the premises full time, we'd be able to smooth out any differences, But as Jerry grew more distant with me, it became obvious that Leslie was pulling his strings. I'd occasionally run into her ex-husband around town so one day I asked him for the straight story on her. He told me they had never officially divorced, that she had a drug problem, had been in jail several times, and had had federal warrants issued against her for her role in an investment scam. I'd also see a few of Leslie's cousins from time to time and they confirmed her ex-husband's account. I knew Jerry wouldn't react well if I directly confronted him, so I tried to plant seeds whenever I could. I'd ask things like "Has Leslie ever been married before?" and "Has she ever been in trouble with the law?" Unfortunately, the subtle approach didn't work; our relationship continued to deteriorate. Worse yet, I feared that Jerry and Leslie, who had both struggled with substance abuse, were back to using drugs again. But even with all that turmoil going on, we were still delivering quality products and the business was doing well.

By June 1997, Jerry had married Leslie and she had escalated her efforts to turn him against me. She had pounced on the check incident and relentlessly used it as ammunition against me. "See, I told you he's trying to screw you," she told Jerry. "He's going to take everything from you. We don't need him. I can run things better than he can." That explains why Jerry kept hammering away at me about the check misunderstanding every chance he could. His obsession with it was all the evidence I needed that he was messing with drugs again. Just like when he had been using years ago, he was becoming increasingly suspicious and paranoid.

Now that Jerry and Leslie were married, our conflicts at work, as well as Jerry himself, quickly spiraled out of control. Jerry would often come to work smelling of alcohol; he'd tell people that the cup he carried around all day was filled with water but it was pure vodka. As the weeks rolled by, he became increasingly difficult to work with.

The tough part about all this was I didn't have anyone to talk to about what was going on with Jerry and me. I couldn't vent to my mom and dad because I'd be talking about their son. All my friends and relatives also knew Jerry so there was nobody to turn to. I felt very alone. And the deeper that Leslie sunk her hooks into him, the more our relationship disintegrated.

Finally, in August 1997, it became clear, even to my father, who had retired recently and was coming in every day to help out, that one of us had to go. Our dad couldn't stand seeing his two sons bickering and butting heads every day. He told us, "Look, you two just can't work together. One of you should buy the other one out." Jerry and I agreed that my dad was right. In fact, it sounded great to me because I knew I'd be fine either way; if Jerry bought me out I'd just set up another company. I suggested to Jerry that we both write down the dollar amount of what we thought the company was worth. When we revealed what we had jotted down, both figures were around $50,000, which was essentially the value of the inventory on hand. I said, "Great, you wanna buy me out then?" Jerry said, "Well, no, I thought you were gonna buy *me* out." I said, "Well, if that's what you want, sure, I'll do that." When we drew up the papers, I didn't include a non-compete agreement. I didn't want to hold my brother back from making a living.

Sure enough, Jerry and Leslie moved to Minneapolis and started a company that did exactly what Advanced Lighting did. Initially, they had some success, primarily because Jerry "confided" in my customers about what an evil guy I was and how I had forced him out of the business. They even snowed Tony at Rose Brand, a distributor of custom stage curtains and one of my best customers. Over time, however, Tony and others came to realize that Jerry's story didn't measure up. Rose Brand, for instance, had begun alternating their orders between Jerry's company and mine. I continued to deliver quality products professionally and on time, whereas Leslie would routinely call Tony and say, "We need to get paid now or we can't build your product." Tony would point out that he had already given them a 50 percent deposit but Leslie would insist on getting more. What Jerry and Leslie really needed money for was drugs; they began evading their financial obligations by moving their operations from building to building and stringing along their vendors. It didn't take Tony long to recognize that something was amiss. When Tony asked me about it, I didn't speak ill of Jerry. I just said, "My brother's a great guy, but he's going through a really hard time so I'm glad you're giving him some business. His wife's another story, but I'll leave that for you to judge." Within a year, Tony told me he couldn't work with Leslie anymore, and like all the companies that had shifted some of their orders to Jerry's company, Rose Brand gave all their business back to Advanced Lighting. Tony apologized to me, saying, "We're really sorry for misjudging you. Your brother needs to get his act together and that wife of his is crazy." Tony was a stand-up guy. Years later, I saw him at a trade show and he asked me how Jerry and my parents were doing. He had met them when he had come to Minnesota to visit our plant and he was genuinely concerned for their well-being. He said he hoped that Jerry had turned his life around and that he wished him the best.

A year and a half after marrying Leslie, Jerry got nailed for a DUI. He was sent to a treatment center for a month and then to a halfway house for another month. During that time, Leslie drained their business account and hit the road. She didn't get far. A cop pulled her over and found drugs and ten grand in cash in her car; she was also using stolen license tabs. The police impounded the car, called me and said, "We've got your wife." Puzzled, I said, "I'm not married." The officer said, "Well, Leslie Streitz says she's married to Paul Streitz and the car is in your name. You're saying she's not your wife?" I said, "She's my brother's wife. Furthermore, they owe me money on that car." When Jerry and I had parted ways, we agreed that he could take the company car as long as he made the payments on it. He had made a few payments but then stopped, which put me on the hook because the car was still in my name and I didn't want my credit trashed. Once I got things straightened out with the police and purchased insurance for the car, since Jerry and Leslie had let it lapse, I went down to the impound lot to claim it. I was in for a shock. In six months that car went from brand-new to torn apart.

Jerry's stint in rehab seemed to do everything my family hoped it would do for him. He sobered up, split with Leslie, and started to get his life in order. Unfortunately, his metamorphosis didn't last long because he was still thinking like a victim. Our relationship hadn't rebounded because he had convinced himself that I had stolen that thousand dollars and had pushed him out of the company. Before long, he was using drugs again, and had sunk even further than he had before. He started stuttering and mumbling like Ozzy Osbourne; it was sickening to see him so brain-fried. In 2002, he was arrested on drug charges and sent to prison for five years.

Even in the worst of times I still loved my brother, but I was so angry at Jerry that it took me two years to visit him in jail. My resentment had nothing to do with business; it was because he had hurt my parents so much. The worse he had behaved, the more they suffered. Finally, my girlfriend Krissy persuaded me to go see him in the lockup. I was amazed to find that he was a very different man than the one who had entered prison. His head had cleared and he was starting to own up to his mistakes. By the time he was released, he had a new attitude and a new resolve to make a better life for himself. I guess you have a lot of time to think when you're in the slammer.

When Jerry got out of prison, he apologized to everyone and did his best to make things right with our family. He was like a little puppy dog, knowing he had done wrong. He told me, "I know I could've been a part of something really big and my problems got in the way of that. I don't hold a grudge toward you anymore, Paul. I understand where you were coming from."

It felt good to have my brother back. A few years after leaving prison, Jerry needed a place to live so I invited him to move in with me. He's the same giving, loving person he used to be, and the bond between us now is as strong as it ever was. Even so, it hasn't been easy for Jerry. He was diagnosed with bipolar disorder and experiences chronic pain from a back injury he sustained years ago in the military. But what's most important is that we're a family again; and in the end, that's all that really matters.

Blood Is Thicker Than Business
Your Life, Your Thoughts

- What are the benefits of working with a family member or good friend?

- What are the drawbacks of working with a family member or good friend?

- What conditions have to be just right in order for such an arrangement to work well?

- What are three reasons why it's a good idea to put agreements between family members or friends in writing?

- If you've ever had a falling out with loved ones over business or financial issues, what did you learn from the experience?

- What might the repercussions be if you talk ill about a family member or friend who you're having difficulties with?

- Why is it a good idea to remain positive and non-judgmental with others about the rift between you and your loved one.

- If you're angry with a loved one who seems incapable of understanding your point of view, what can you do to work through your anger unilaterally?

- If you are on the outs with a family member or friend, what step can you take right now to begin repairing the damage?

GROWING PAINS

Shortly after we incorporated Advanced Lighting, we hired a woman named Dora to manage the office and do the bookkeeping. It didn't take long to realize that Dora wasn't as competent as we had hoped. Wrong products were shipped to wrong customers, UPS slips were filled out incorrectly, bookkeeping errors were frequent. All these little problems added up to a big problem: We were a young company trying to grow, and I was spending way too much time and attention stamping out fires caused by Dora's mistakes.

One Friday Jerry finally asked me, "What's up with Dora? There are a lot of mistakes going on." I said, "I know, and I don't know what to do about it." He said, "Well, you're the business manager. I run the shop. It's your job to get rid of her." He was right and I knew it. I told Jerry I'd take care of it on Monday.

All weekend long, I dreaded the thought of confronting Dora. When I walked in the office on Monday morning, she cheerfully asked me how my weekend was and I chickened out. I couldn't pull the trigger the next day either, or the day after that. I had always respected older people, and Dora was so sweet and nice that I just couldn't stand the thought of ruining her life. Every day that I procrastinated made me feel that much worse. At night I tossed and turned and couldn't sleep. I felt sick about what I had to do. Meanwhile, the problems weren't going away; if anything, she was making even more mistakes.

Then one day, a couple of customers called complaining that their orders were messed up, and I knew I had to man up. I walked over and said, "Dora, what's going on?" She looked at me blankly and said, "What do you mean?" I showed her the invoices and shipping records and pointed out her errors. She looked at me and said, "I suppose I'm fired, huh?" I said, "Well, to be honest, there's been a ton of mistakes the last couple months and we just can't afford to have this going on." She nodded and said, "I understand, Paul, I totally understand." I said, "It's not that we don't care about you, but you have to understand that these things just have to be right." She nodded again. I said, "Dora, I feel terrible. This is the first time I ever had to let someone go." She smiled, stood up, and gave me a hug. She said, "Paul, it'll be okay. I'll find another job. Life goes on. You're a great person and I've enjoyed working for you. I've learned so much and I hope you're okay." After Dora left, I fell back in my chair and exhaled for what felt like the first time in two weeks. I was so relieved that Dora wasn't upset. In fact, she seemed relieved herself. I think she knew deep down that she wasn't getting the job done.

Letting Dora go prompted me to do some soul-searching. I knew I'd be faced with similar situations in the future and I didn't want to be a nervous wreck every time I had to show someone the door. Filling Dora's position hadn't been the problem because it wasn't a difficult job to replace. It was all about the human factor; Dora had a husband and kids, and her family needed a steady paycheck. I didn't want her or anybody else who worked for me to endure a financial hardship, even if they had put themselves in that position because of poor performance.

I got another flash of insight when Dora hugged me goodbye. For a moment, my mind raced back to the fifth grade when I had been rejected by two of my Cub Scout friends. I remember feeling an almost desperate craving for acceptance after that incident, which came on the heels of abuse I had suffered at the hands of bullies (see the "Summer of Shame" chapter for the full story). That unreasonable need to be liked by everyone at all times was still plaguing me all these years later.

Intellectually, I knew it wasn't realistic to take responsibility for someone else's financial well-being or to expect that I could please everybody. But that didn't make it any easier to work through those issues and get past them. Old patterns of thinking and feeling can be hard to uproot and replace. Ultimately, I realized that the only way to serve the best interests of both my business and the people who worked for me was to be tough-minded but kind-hearted. Once I achieved that balance of being firm yet compassionate, I could let go of the need to control how people felt about me and trust that they could take care of their own emotional and financial needs.

Dora was the perfect example of how well that management style worked. If I had been tough-minded without being compassionate, our final encounter would have been far less pleasant because I wouldn't have been honoring her as someone worthy of respect. If I had been less firm and too kind-hearted, I would have put what I thought were her needs over the needs of the company. As it turned out, I was wrong about her needs. She was far more resilient than I gave her credit for and I certainly didn't ruin her life. By taking a tough-minded but kind-hearted approach, we were able to end the relationship with mutual respect and admiration. And I had the satisfaction of knowing that I treated Dora as well as I would have liked to be treated had our situations been reversed.

I also took a look in the mirror and admitted that if anyone was to blame for Dora's inability to do the job, it was me. She was good-hearted and well-intentioned, but she simply wasn't qualified for the position. If I had been clearer about what was expected of her before I hired her, Dora would have had the opportunity to say, "You know, Paul, I'll be on time and I'm great at answering the phones. I'm probably not as proficient in accounting as you want me to be, but I'm willing to work hard and learn." At that point I could have said, "Maybe this isn't the right position for you, Dora. We can only afford to hire one person and we need that person to be experienced in accounting." If I had covered the basics like that, I could have averted the whole uncomfortable experience of having to fire her.

I see now that I did what many small business owners probably do: I hired up to my own psychological limitations. Even though I had confidence in our products and capabilities, there was a lot of uncertainty about how successful the company would ultimately be. I was willing to risk everything to chase after my dream but was insecure about asking others to go all in, especially people who were already successful and who had a lot more to lose than lower-level employees like Dora did. If I hired super-talented people who gave up secure, well-paying positions to join our company, I'd feel a lot worse if we ended up going under and dragging them down with us. That was a lot of responsibility for me to shoulder and I wasn't ready to handle it yet.

I graduated to the big leagues when I built Advanced Lighting's new headquarters in 1999. I knew I needed a *real* controller, somebody who'd be able to look me in the eye and say, "No, Paul, *this* is the way it needs to be done." I made room in the budget for a big salary and put the word out that I was looking for top-notch candidates. I remember looking through the resumes that came in and thinking, *God, all these people have degrees and they're so much smarter than I am. I must be awfully arrogant to expect them to leave a sure thing for my company.* It was a big hurdle for me to ask someone to take a leap of faith in something that I was insecure about myself. Yet I knew deep down that if I was going to be successful, I had to surround myself with people who were better and more experienced than me in every aspect of the business.

Hiring Marlon as our head bean counter was just the remedy I needed. He was my direct opposite in pretty much every way but he was perfect for the company. When I'd go flying off into Idea Land, he'd reel me back down to solid ground. Even though Marlon relieved me of the pressure that came with managing our finances, I felt even more pressure overall. I had just built a new building and taken on more employees and more overhead. If everything blew up, I knew I had the resources to find another job or start another business. But it wasn't just about me anymore; other people were putting their families, mortgages, and car payments in my hands, trusting that I had something good going. I had to show up—big time. I had to make this thing happen.

Adding Marlon was pivotal. It was like breaking through a barrier that I had constructed myself. Marlon was the first degreed professional to join the company. Hiring the next one was easier. Welcoming these all-stars to our team was incredibly motivating. By coming on board, they were saying that they believed in me, that they trusted me to lead them. That made me feel both humbled and empowered, and it lit a burning fire inside me to do right by them.

A couple of years earlier, I had gotten my first inkling of what was at stake. I had needed to drop something off for Karen, our head seamstress, so I drove over to her house. Sauk Centre is a small town and it was common for people just to drop by to say hi. Karen said her husband and son were out hunting for the weekend. While we were chatting, she pointed out the window and said, "See that camper out there, Paul? That's because of you. We make enough money now that my husband and son can take a little time off from work and go hunting. And that's because of you too. And I appreciate it." Wow. I left feeling like a million bucks. Knowing that I was making a difference in a family's life like that was so gratifying. And knowing that my employees believed in me helped me believe in myself even more.

I got along great with my employees because I never lost sight of the fact that the people who worked for me were human beings first and employees second. I have to admit, though, that that attitude was sorely tested when Karen started going through menopause shortly after her camper comment. She'd be at her sewing machine and either be dripping sweat or freezing or crying so hard that we had to keep feeding her boxes of Kleenex. We all did our best to comfort and support her. This went on for a full year. Karen was such a mess on some days that she had to leave early. But that was okay. I talked to my mom and other women about what to expect, which helped me be more sympathetic to what she was going through.

Our company was built on rush projects, and even though Karen was a daily drama just waiting to happen, she always delivered in a weird, roundabout way and never missed a deadline. Until, that is, the day she disappeared. I asked her coworkers where she went and was told, "I don't know. She was crying and just left." I figured she just needed a break. The next day, I got her resignation letter in the mail. I was stunned. My first thought was, *What did I do wrong?* I paid her well and had always respected her. In fact, I had treated her even better over the last year because I knew she was going through a tough time. I felt hurt that she left me in the lurch like that without so much of a word of explanation. I was also instantly stressed out because we had a ton of jobs in the hopper and I didn't have anyone to replace her. It wasn't easy to find people who could sew huge 30' x 60' theatrical curtains.

I immediately hopped in my car and headed over to Karen's house to try to talk her out of it. She wasn't home. I was in such distress that I went through a stop sign on the way back to the office and got pulled over by a cop. When he told me I was also speeding, I said, "I'm sure I was." I told him that a very important employee had just quit and I was freaking out. He nodded in sympathy and said, "Tell you what. I'll just write you a ticket for going a couple miles over the limit." I thanked him and drove back to work, wondering what I was going to tell my customers whose orders wouldn't be done on time.

I didn't sleep too well that night, but the very next day, a middle-aged woman showed up out of nowhere and said, "I've been a seamstress all my life. My husband and I are going through some financial difficulties and I need a job." I said, "Well, there's a machine; do you think you can sew huge stage curtains?" She said, "Let me show you," and she zipped right through a sample. She was just as good, if not better than, Karen. I thought, *Wow, it's funny how life works.* Our new seamstress got every job out on time and I didn't lose any more sleep.

Nine months later, I noticed that our building was preparing a space for a new tenant called Stage Left. I also noticed that my chattering employees were clamming up whenever I'd walk by. I finally said, "Okay, guys, what's going on?" One of them blurted out, "Karen just started a staging company. She's making fiber optic curtains just like we are. We're going to go out of business." They were worried because we were in a unique industry and thought we were vulnerable because we had only one other direct competitor in all of North America. I laughed and said, "Don't worry about it. First of all, we're not going go out of business. Second, all of our customers are very loyal. And third, all Karen knows is sewing. She has to learn everything else that you do and I do and everybody else does. We're already that far ahead of her. All we can do is hold our heads high, wish her the best of luck, and be a tough competitor."

Until we moved into our new headquarters eighteen months later, Stage Left and Advanced Lighting operated out of the same warehouse. Karen had her own separate entrance and hallway on the opposite end of the building and I never ran into her. A decade later, Stage Left still exists. I heard through mutual friends that Karen had resigned from Advanced Lighting because she couldn't handle the stress of our deadlines. I was glad to learn that she had quit over something that had nothing to do with me. From what I hear, she's happy that she's working for herself, can do things her own way, keep her company small, and avoid situations that would overwhelm her. I can certainly respect that. Ultimately, everything worked out great. I found a replacement, Karen found peace and happiness, and Advanced Lighting never skipped a beat. Everybody won.

Growing Pains
Your Life, Your Thoughts

- How do you balance the best interests of an organization with the best interests of the individuals working there?

- In what ways are you helping and hurting an employee if you keep them on despite their inability to do the job?

- What place do kindness and compassion have in the workplace?

- Why is being tough-minded but kind-hearted the ideal workplace attitude?

- How can you do a better job of putting people in the best possible position to succeed?

- What fears and insecurities do you bring into the workplace from your personal life and how do those issues affect your business decisions?

- If you're feeling too much pressure and stress at work, how can you develop a healthier perspective?

- What services can you have in place at work to help employees who are experiencing personal difficulties?

- In what ways do your competitors help your business?

BROADWAY SNAFU

In the spring of 1998, Advanced Lighting received an order for a $40,000 fiber optic curtain for the Washington D.C. opening of the musical *Ragtime*. I enjoyed working on high-profile jobs like this, but when we received the technical blueprints I saw nothing but red flags.

Typically, a 30' x 60' stage-show curtain is embedded with thousands of points of light. It's a complex job because the placement of each light has to be precise. The lights on the *Ragtime* curtain needed to form a variety of star constellations as well as spell out the name of the show. While this particular curtain called for 30 percent less lights than normal, the show's lighting designer was asking for glass fibers, which were roughly five times heavier than the industry-standard plastic. We had experimented with glass fibers in the past but determined that they were just too heavy for detailed work. Plastic is not only lighter, it's more durable and flexible, which is especially important if you want to fold up a curtain and take it on tour.

I immediately called Rose Brand and told Tony, my contact there, that the curtain they ordered was a disaster waiting to happen. I explained that the glass and adhesives would be so heavy that the curtain would almost certainly rip. Tony relayed my message to the show's lighting designer, Jules Fisher, who replied, "No, no, no, it's got to be glass fiber." Obviously, someone had convinced him that glass fiber was superior to plastic, which, in favorable circumstances, is true. Glass fiber is awesome if you're talking about a 30' x 40' curtain with a couple of thousand fibers. But when you add twenty feet of curtain and many more thousands of fibers, you're asking for trouble.

I told Tony that we couldn't make the curtain because our reputation was on the line; I didn't want our name associated with what could potentially be a nightmare scenario. But word came back to me that Jules was insisting on his original specs. If it had been any other designer and any other distributor, I wouldn't have budged. But Jules was a repeat customer and the number-one guy in the industry; at the time, he had won seven Tony awards for lighting design, more than anyone else in history. Just as importantly, Rose Brand was the premier player in Broadway theatrical curtains and one of our biggest and best customers. If I walked away from this job, I'd be walking away from a steady diet of big-ticket jobs from two of my best customers. I finally told

Tony, "Okay, look, we'll build the curtain but we're not accepting any liability for it. If Jules is willing to sign off on that, we're fine." Tony said, "Sure, that's no problem. Everything's understood."

Now came the hard part. Plastic fiber came in spools of ten thousand feet; you just spool off what you need and you're good to go. Glass fiber, on the other hand, is made to order. It took me a week to figure out the placement of every last point on the curtain and calculate all the necessary lengths and angles. I figured we'd have plenty of time to assemble the curtain but I started sweating a bit more every day our glass-fiber order was delayed from the manufacturer. We finally got the glass on a Monday—two weeks late!—and the curtain had to be *delivered and in place* on the East coast by that Friday for their first dress rehearsal. If that wasn't intense enough, not only did we have to affix fifteen thousand fibers, we had to give the adhesive twenty-four hours to dry. My crew, God bless 'em, worked two straight sixteen hour days, kicked ass, and got that bad boy done. It was such an important job that we folded it up and I flew to D.C. with it.

When I got to the theater, everyone raved about how fantastic the curtain looked. Relieved, I plopped down next to Jules Fisher to watch the stagehands install the curtain and hoist it up to the ceiling, where it would be lowered for several scenes during the show. The crew pulled the curtain up and dropped it back down to test it. As soon as it hit the floor, it jerked once . . . and ripped apart.

Everyone froze. When my heart started beating again, my mind began racing with three thoughts. First, I thought I should run up on stage for appearances' sake and assess the damage even though I knew the curtain was toast. Second, I was hoping Jules wouldn't slug me. Third, I had an overwhelming urge to jump up and bolt out the door. It took a few seconds to realize that all eyes were on me, waiting for me to take action. So I sprang up, ran onstage, and went through the motions of checking out the curtain. I already knew the curtain wasn't salvageable but running my hands over it and pretending to look for a solution gave me a few minutes to compose myself. When Jules finally broke the silence by saying, "Can you fix it?" I felt like a doctor answering a terminally ill patient. "There's nothing we can do," I said gravely. "We'd have to start all over and do it with plastic; glass just weighs too much." I paused for dramatic effect—after all, I was onstage—and added, "That was my fear." Fortunately, Jules remained relatively calm. He said, "Well, we need to get a curtain made and we need it here by the end of next week." I nodded and said, "Let me get on the phone with Rose Brand."

As I was dialing Rose Brand's number, the enormity of what had just happened hit me full force and I fought off a wave of panic. All sorts of crazy thoughts started roaring through my head. This was a $40,000 job that had turned to ashes, and for all I knew, my company could turn to ashes too. Not only was this a significant amount of money, it could also bring our reputation crashing down. Plus, making a replacement curtain was no slam dunk. I wasn't completely sure that we had enough plastic fiber in inventory or that we weren't already booked solid with other rush jobs.

When Tony answered the phone, I said, "We've got a problem." Tony and I had a longstanding, friendly relationship and I knew I could speak candidly with him. I told him the curtain had shredded, which was exactly what I had warned could happen. To my surprise, Tony just said, "Well, you took the job." I said, "Wait a minute, we talked about this. I said we'd only do the job if we wouldn't be held liable if it didn't work." I hadn't insisted on getting our agreement in writing because, given the solid business relationships I had with Tony and Jules, I expected them to honor their word should anything happen. But as we continued talking, and Tony continued hemming and hawing, I saw that Tony was caught in the crossfire. Jules Fisher did a significant amount of business with Rose Brand and Tony didn't feel he was in a position to make any demands of Jules. That meant Rose Brand would be on the hook for the full forty grand, and Tony was understandably uncomfortable about telling his bosses that he had agreed to a deal that had blown up in his face. Clearly, that wasn't my fault, but that didn't stop it from becoming my problem.

Frustrated and upset, I hung up. I was right, and Tony knew it, but that didn't mean I'd ever see a penny in payment. Given that my motto is, "There's always a way to work things out," I sat down and began brainstorming. Yes, I was out $40,000, but my real costs in parts and labor was closer to $25,000. I added up all the jobs we'd done with Jules Fisher and Rose Brand and came up with a figure north of $2 million. This was our first major foul-up with any client, so from a percentage standpoint we were still ahead of the game. We were also in a good cash position at the time. So even though it stung big time to take a hit like this, I figured the best strategy was to eat the loss, swallow it along with my pride, and make the best of what I had to work with.

As I did the math on the specs for a new curtain, a plan started taking shape in my mind. First, I asked Rose Brand to donate the fabric and sewing for the new curtain and pick up the overnight freight charges, which saved a few thousand bucks. Next, I asked my employees to help out with another rush job and to put in overtime hours at their regular hourly rate. Given that plastic fiber was less expensive than glass and I could re-use the fourteen illuminators (which lit up the fiber) from the original curtain, Operation Ragtime Rescue kicked into high gear. Three days later, Jules had his curtain in time for the grand opening that night and I looked like a hero.

With the concessions from Rose Brand and my crew, the replacement curtain had cost only another ten grand, bringing my total cost for both curtains to $35,000. I got paid $40,000 so I didn't end up losing a nickel. More importantly, I not only salvaged my relationships with Jules and Tony, they were stronger than ever because I saved the day without making them look bad. In fact, the president of Rose

Brand called me to thank me for making them look great in a bad situation, which was a very gentlemanly thing to do. And I think Jules did even more business with me because he appreciated that I took the high road and acted honorably. And the more business we did with Jules, including producing curtains for four of his Tony Award-winning shows, the more business we got from other Broadway designers. After all, everyone wants to follow the leader.

Looking back, I think I would have done the same thing even if I had had our agreement in writing. Being less concerned with being right than with doing the right thing is just smart business. Sure, I could have sued a multimillion-dollar theatrical company and a nationally respected Tony Award winner, but even if I had won I would have lost. My legal costs would have eaten up my profits and then some and I never would have gotten another job from either of them again. On top of all that, a big chunk of my mental focus and energy would've been poured into a soul-sucking black hole of negativity for God knows how long. Instead, I invested another ten grand and got the forty grand that was due me. All things considered, that was quite the bargain.

Broadway Snafu
Your Life, Your Thoughts

- How willing are you to proceed with a project in the midst of red flags in order to preserve an important relationship?

- In what circumstances can a signed contract do more harm than good?

- How far are you willing to go to keep your best customer?

- What are two keys to overcoming a stalemate with a good customer?

- Why is it important to do the right thing even when you feel you've been wronged?

- What are three things you can do this week to improve your relationships with your best customers?

FROM RUSSIA, WITH GOUT

I was happy to make it to Russia in one piece. I had flown from Minneapolis to Frankfurt in December 2003 before catching an Aeroflot flight to Moscow, where the two-day Intertech trade show was being held. Aeroflot is the largest Russian airline but the plane was a little too rickety for my comfort. It didn't help that it was cold and snowy and we were fighting turbulence most of the way.

Ivan, my Russian distributor, was waiting for me as I got off the plane. He obviously had some pull, because just like my airport experience in Mexico fifteen years earlier, I was led right past the line of people waiting to go through customs. The customs official stamped my passport, waved me on through, and away we went. After a few minutes on the highway, I was still cold as hell so I asked Ivan to turn up the heat. He laughed and said, "This is Moscow. We like cold weather." I felt like saying, "Hey, buddy, I'm from Minnesota. I'm no slouch in the cold department but this mother is freezing!" I was shivering all the way to my hotel. Before I jumped out of the car, Ivan said he'd pick me up at nine in the morning. I shouted, "Okay!" and ran into the warm lobby.

The next morning, Ivan's ice-mobile pulled up precisely at nine. I had made a point to fly in Wednesday night so I could visit his company's headquarters on Thursday morning. They were nice offices, nothing fancy, and looked like a typical business in the United States. Ivan gave me a tour and we spent some time preparing for the lighting trade show that started in two days. Ivan said, "Tonight we're going to meet the client we did a half-a-million-dollar job for. I think you're going to find it very special." I said, "Great! I love meeting customers." That afternoon, he drove me back to the hotel and waited in the lobby while I got ready. We had to dress up because the client in question was Casino Mirage, an upscale European-type casino that took up a city block in the heart of Moscow. After arriving at the casino, we roamed around admiring the lighting displays we had manufactured and installed there. I was proud of the job we had done because it had been a massive undertaking. We later featured the casino interior on our website and in our print literature.

At the appointed time, Ivan led the way to the restaurant, which was over-the-top luxurious. Shortly after Ivan and I arrived, the casino manager and a handful of his associates joined us. Twenty minutes later, the casino owner made his grand entrance, accompanied by security and two sexy young women (because, you know, one's not enough and three is too many). The host presented us with menus and supervised the arrangement of glistening steel buckets on elegant stands, which I assumed were for chilled bottles of wine or champagne. Silly me; this was Russia. Out came four bottles of vodka. I wasn't a big vodka fan, or even much of a drinker, so I felt a bit uncomfortable. But you know what they say: When in Russia, do as the Russians do. I just went with the flow when it came time to order salad and soup too. I didn't have a clue what the choices were so when Ivan insisted I try the asparagus soup, I said sure. Whoa. Potent stuff. The rest of the meal was pleasant but uneventful.

After saying our goodbyes, I decided to gamble a bit and sat down at a blackjack table. A middle-aged guy next to me struck up a conversation by asking if I was from America. He then introduced me to his handsome young son, who said he lived in Vegas and was the star of Zumanity, the Cirque du Soleil show at the New York, New York hotel. "Wow, small world," I said. "I provided you guys with your backdrop, the one with the little lights and stars." He said, "Oh, yes, that backdrop is beautiful, but the performers do not like it." When I asked why, he explained that the actors kept getting scratched by the fiber optics because they're half naked during the show. We had a good laugh about that. At that point, Ivan, who didn't gamble, motioned for us to get going.

As Ivan and I were walking back to the car, a policeman stopped us and, knowing I was a foreigner, asked me for my papers. Immediately, my mind flashed to movies I'd seen where a uniformed authority figure in a foreign country stops the hero and demands to see his papers. It was a surreal moment, but in a weird way it felt a little cool too, like I was in a movie myself. Before I could respond, Ivan, who looked more Italian then Russian, got up in the guy's face and unleashed a torrent of Russian profanity. The police officer timidly handed back my passport and hurried off. Ivan explained that rogue cops make good money on the side by asking for tourists' papers and then making them buy their passports back at the threat of getting locked up. I was lucky to have dodged a bullet.

Ivan also told me about another scam that I later learned a pilot friend of mine had fallen prey to. He had been walking on a busy sidewalk in Moscow when the guy in front of him dropped his wallet. Naturally, my friend picked up the wallet, tapped the guy on the shoulder and said, "Excuse me, sir, you dropped this." Boom! A rogue cop was all over him, accusing him of stealing the guy's wallet. He threatened to take my friend to jail unless he paid him "restitution," which I guess is the Russian way to spell "extortion." Since he didn't have much cash on him, he was hauled off to jail. He called the hotel and got hold of a fellow pilot who came down to the jail and paid off the police.

Getting stopped by the cop was a good reminder to be careful and keep my antennae up. After Ivan dropped me off at my hotel and said he'd pick me up at ten the next morning, I thought, *What the hell. It's still early, I'm gonna go out.* I asked the concierge for a recommendation and he sent me to a nearby café that served typical American fare like hamburgers and fries. It turned out to be a terrific place, with a live band and tons of people. The big surprise was that it was teeming with drop-dead gorgeous women who kept asking me to dance. I thought, *Man, these Russian girls sure are friendly!* It wasn't until I was talking with a few American guys at the bar that I learned they were working girls. I was shocked. I later asked one of the women why she was doing that kind of work. She just shrugged and said there wasn't much opportunity in Russia and it was how they survived. Man, what a way to earn a living. After a couple of hours there, I took a taxi back to the hotel.

At 7 AM I woke up shouting, "Oh, my God! What happened?" I whipped off the sheet and stared at my right foot. The weight of the sheet on my foot had been enough to leave me gasping with pain. My foot was a little red, but it wasn't swollen or discolored. I flashed back to the night before but couldn't remember bumping or banging into anything. I thought maybe I had jammed my right toe but when I tried to touch it, it was so hyper-sensitive that I yelped at the slightest touch. I laid back down and tried to keep still, but even then I'd feel a sharp, stabbing sensation every few seconds.

When Ivan called to say he was on his way, I told him, "I've got a problem. Something happened to my foot and I don't know what's going on." Fifteen minutes later when Ivan knocked on my door, I had to crawl over to let him in. He immediately called the desk and asked them to send the hotel doctor up. The medic looked at my foot and said I better get to a hospital. When I muttered something about not wanting to go to a Russian hospital, he assured me, "No, the international hospitals are good here." The medic left and returned with some crutches, so I got dressed and hobbled down to Ivan's car in the winter cold with my right foot bare. After waiting a half hour at the hospital, which looked more like a sterile, nondescript government office, a French doctor came in to examine me. She poked my toe and took X-rays, but admitted she was stumped. She tried wrapping my foot but I couldn't take the pressure, so she told me to return to the hotel and elevate my foot. On the way back to the hotel, Ivan said, "The trade show starts tomorrow, but I don't think you'll be able to do it." I agreed, but held out hope that my toe would improve enough over the next couple of days to allow me to at least spend some time at the show.

Sitting around my hotel room all day was maddening, especially because I didn't know what the hell had happened to me. And then it hit me: I remembered my dad complaining of pain like this six months earlier. He had a horrible case of gout and had told me that the weight of the sheet on his foot was enough to send him through the roof. I grabbed the phone and called him. Thank God he answered. I said, "Dad, I'm okay, but I'm in Russia and I hurt my foot. You told me about having gout not long ago. What did that feel like?" Everything he told me perfectly described what I was experiencing. I hated the thought of having gout but I was glad to have figured out what was wrong. He told me that gout is usually food-related and it's a buildup of uric acid that makes you feel like you've got pins and needles in your joints. When I asked him what kinds of foods he was talking about, he said he had to watch out for green beans, asparagus, spinach, or too much red meat. I said, "Wait a minute; asparagus? I had a fermented asparagus soup last night." He said, "Well, I betcha that's what did it, Paul. The good news is, gout goes away on its own. Sometimes mine goes away overnight and sometimes it takes four or five days. The best thing you can do is drink lots of fluids, especially fruit juice." Here I had seen two medical professionals who didn't have a clue, and it's Doctor Dad who came to the rescue!

I immediately ordered tons of fruit juice from room service and guzzled them the rest of the day. I went to sleep that night with my foot outside of the sheets and woke up the next morning feeling 80 percent better. I still had to be careful but I was thrilled that I could put on a shoe! I called Ivan and surprised him by telling him I was good to go. A couple of times during the trade show I had to take my shoe off and sit down for a while, but I was able to be on my feet most of the day. I was fine the next day too, and had a fun time promoting my products and schmoozing with prospects at our booth. That night, I joined Ivan for a fancy farewell dinner with his employees to thank them for their hard work. Ivan, who knew I was going to be in Russia for one more day, told me that his partner, Dmitry, would be happy to show me the sights around Moscow on

Monday. Dmitry shook my hand and said, "Whatever you'd like to do, just let me know. Ivan chose me because I'm more extravagant than he is. I can tell that you like nice things and I enjoy doing this."

Dmitry and I had a great time being tourists the next day. He showed me all the hot spots around town, I did some shopping, and we toured the Kremlin and Red Square. A little before eleven o'clock, I came across a spot in Red Square that was the perfect vantage point for a photo of the whole area so I whipped out my digital camera and got a great shot. The next day, I flew to Frankfurt, Germany, to visit my first cousin. It was the last leg of my trip and my foot was doing much better so I was looking forward to seeing her and her husband. I rented a car at the airport and drove the hundred miles to my hotel in Cologne. After checking in, I turned on CNN and saw the breaking news that a female suicide bomber had set off an explosive belt in Red Square that morning, killing six people and injuring dozens. I grabbed my digital camera and looked at the photo I had taken and the time-stamp on it. A chill ran up my spine when I saw that the bomb had been detonated at the exact same spot at the exact same time I had taken that photo just twenty-four hours earlier. I was pretty shaken up the rest of the day.

It's been seven years since that trip, but every time I think of how close I came to leaving this earth, I do what I did that day in my hotel room: I count my blessings and send up a prayer of gratitude for being alive.

From Russia, With Gout
Your Life, Your Thoughts

- When traveling in a foreign country, why is it a good idea to have a written-out plan in case of an emergency?

- Does your emergency plan include contact info for the best people to call in different types of situations?

- Does your emergency plan include provisions for notifying your family if you're out of commission?

- Does your health insurance cover you during foreign travel or will you have to buy supplemental insurance?

- How would your attitude and life change if you took a few minutes out of every day to express gratitude for all your many blessings?

POWER PLAY

In the summer of 2006, six years after hiring Marlon as controller at Advanced Lighting, I knew it was time to push beyond my insecurities again and hire someone with a strong background in sales and marketing. We had a good salesman who was acting as the lead guy, but our team agreed we were ready to take a step up in professionalism.

After putting out feelers on lighting industry websites and sorting through the candidates that responded, one candidate stood out: Kelly Jones, a former college professor from Santa Fe. I got Kelly on the phone and was impressed with her smarts. She had a master's degree in business and had extensive experience with strategic planning. She sounded like a perfect fit so I flew her out to Minnesota for an interview.

Kelly and I really hit it off. I remember thinking, *What a great find!* When it came to hiring people,

I didn't have the resources of a large company; I just went with my instincts. Besides, Kelly had a terrific resume, great references, and we had a good rapport.

Kelly and I couldn't have gotten off to a better start. She was very social, active in the community, and made a lot of friends. Work-wise, she came as advertised. She was sharp and savvy and her strategic planning skills were invaluable. The industry measurements and benchmarks she put together helped keep me grounded instead of flying by the seat of my pants. We had a great working relationship, and everything rolled along smoothly for the first few months. Every so often, she'd tell me in an e-mail what a great leader I was. I'd return the compliment and tell her she was doing a great job too.

I welcomed Kelly's input on every aspect of the business. I told her, "Yes, I may own the company but that doesn't mean I'm always right. As long as the ideas you present to me are well thought out and you explain all the pros and cons, I'm open to making changes and adjustments. That's why you're here. That doesn't mean I'm going to go with every suggestion you make, but I do want to hear what you're thinking and I'll never hold it against you if you respectfully disagree with me."

Around the first of the year in 2007, I got a call that every entrepreneur dreams of. It was from the CEO of a major player in the industry. He essentially said, "You know us, we know you, we've been friendly competitors for quite a while. What do you think of merging our companies?" The question caught me off guard. All I could say was, "Well, that sounds interesting. What exactly are you thinking and what would that look like?" Over the next two months, as discussions heated up, I signed some confidentiality agreements and started to think, *Wow, this could really happen.* Finally, we got to the point where I needed to bring in my attorney, my CPA, and my two internal right-hand people: Marlon, my controller, and Kelly, my sales and marketing specialist. I explained to my team that I had no intention of selling the company if that meant folding our tent and moving. The merger was all about giving us a better opportunity to take the company to the next level.

Kelly was all jazzed up about the news. She told me, "That's fantastic, Paul! You deserve all the success you get. Let me know whatever I can do to help you." It wasn't until many months later that I realized that that was the day she began hatching her master plan.

For the next month or two, our potential acquirer's employees came in to explore every nook and cranny of Advanced Lighting. I was grateful to have an MBA like Kelly on board who could provide all the detailed information they needed during the due diligence process. Since they were a public company, we had to keep the merger quiet until I signed a definitive agreement, which I did in April 2007 at a trade show in New York. We immediately announced the deal to the public and the press during a media event at the show, which was very cool because nobody saw it coming.

The announcement was all over the press the next morning. Priority one was telling my employees the news so they didn't see it on the Internet or hear it from somebody else and get freaked out. I set up a conference call, asked everyone to gather around the speakerphone and explained what had gone down. I heard later that Kelly got everyone pumped up by calling an impromptu meeting and telling everyone what an awesome deal this was for them because we were going to be a bigger company and that meant higher salaries and more benefits. She said all the right things and left everyone feeling great about the announcement.

When I arrived back in Sauk Centre, I had an extra layer of stress to contend with because the acquiring company's bean counters had come to our office for six months to complete their due diligence. I couldn't believe how meticulous they were with looking at every last detail of everything imaginable. I wasn't in the office as much as usual because of frequent business trips, including appointments with my attorney in Minneapolis (two hours away) and my CPA in St. Cloud (forty-five minutes away). During the entire transition, Kelly was patting me on the back and telling me what a great businessman I was. If it had occurred to me to turn and look in the mirror behind me, I would have seen a knife in my back. It wasn't until much later that I learned that Kelly was using my time away to her advantage, slowly and methodically buddying up to employees, setting me up as the bad guy, and promising them that only she had their best interests at heart.

Six months after the merger was announced, the sale of Advanced Lighting was finalized. It didn't take long for me to realize that something was amiss with Kelly. I picked up immediately that she was treating me less respectfully. The change was subtle, but our interactions definitely had a different feel to them.

With the merger finalized, I started accumulating a lot of frequent-flier miles. I made regular visits to our buyer's facilities and was also jetting off to China and other countries to meet with suppliers and distributors. I wasn't thrilled about all the traveling but I was working for somebody else now and they were calling the shots. One other thing was keeping me away from the office: seller's remorse. I wasn't married, I didn't have kids, so for ten years I had doted on Advanced Lighting. I nurtured it and helped it grow through good times and bad. While I didn't regret the merger, it was harder than I thought it would be to turn my company over to a group of strangers. On days when it was difficult to drag myself to the office, I worked from home, an arrangement I had cleared with my new boss.

Unbeknownst to me, spending so much time away from the office played right into Kelly's hands. She had more time with the employees one on one, so she kicked her plan into high gear. People in the office told me much later that she'd zero in on high-value team members and prey on their small-town naïveté by telling them things like, "Look, Paul doesn't even bother coming to work now that he sold the company. He made his million bucks at your expense and doesn't need you anymore. But don't worry, I've got your back. Once I'm in charge, you're gonna make more money because I'm watching out for you and I care about you guys." I didn't figure it out until it was almost too late, but her master plan was to force me out so she could take over. That's why she had been so excited to hear we were merging with a bigger company. Her thought process must have been, *Public company, Paul doesn't have a degree; the board's gonna like me better. I'm gonna run this business some day.*

Now that I've been able to piece together what happened, what bothered me the most was that a third of my twenty employees, most of whom had worked for me for years, bought Kelly's shtick and turned against me. That wasn't just disheartening, it was heartbreaking. It reminded me of the lack of support my people had given me nine years earlier when our bookkeeper's embezzling caused a payroll problem (see the "Balancing the Books" chapter for the full story). I had always done right by these people and had considered them friends. If anyone was trying to take advantage of one of them, I would have stepped in immediately; in fact, I did so on many occasions. Sauk Centre is a small town and word gets around when something's not right. This business was my baby and the people who worked there were like family. When anyone turns on you, it's distressing. But when it's family, man, that's harsh. Either I was fooling myself about the quality of my relationships with my employees or Kelly had world-class persuasion skills.

I was especially hurt by the defection of two key employees. Russ, one of our key production people, was right in the middle of every order, which is why Kelly targeted him first. Russ was devoutly religious, a nice guy, and a hard worker. At first, I didn't trust my instincts when I sensed that I wasn't getting the attention I needed and expected from him. Something had gone awry and I didn't have a clue what it was. Then I started getting the same treatment from Doug, our electronics manager. That hurt even more. Doug and I had been really close and I had helped him out big time during a rough patch in his life. He was an honorable man and had gone out of his way to let me know he appreciated my help and my friendship. So when he started acting distant and giving me empty answers, I felt like I was in the Twilight Zone.

Marlon was the next person to go all Stepford Wives on me. He was respectful and did whatever I asked, but the connection we once had had been snuffed out. So my production guy, my electronics manager, my controller, and a few other employees were all giving me the cold shoulder. It was frustrating, it was maddening, and I had no idea what to do about it.

Granted, not everyone fell for Kelly's spiel. From time to time, someone would tell me that they heard Kelly had done some such thing or the other. I'd ask things like, "Did she do it to you?" and "Do you have the actual e-mail?" The answer was always no, so I had no choice but to dismiss it as water cooler talk. If an employee had come to me with actual evidence, Kelly would have been history by the end of the day.

What was especially brutal, both in terms of Kelly's tactics and the effect they had on my emotional well-being, was her effort to discredit and dispose of my dad and my brother. Even though our acquiring company had a "no nepotism" policy, they had signed off on the merger with the understanding that we'd be keeping both of them on.

My brother, Jerry, had started Advanced Lighting in 1993. I joined him in 1994 and bought him out three years later. We had had a falling out but patched things up a few years later. By the time of the merger, Jerry had been working part-time for Doug, our electronics manager, for a couple of years. When Jerry came on board, I pulled Doug aside and said, "Doug, I want to make it clear that you're Jerry's boss. There's no sibling favoritism here. If he's doing well, let him know. If he's not working out, let him go. But be direct with him. As long as it's work-related, nothing you're going to say to him is going to bother me. I trust and respect you." Doug asked if I was sure and I told him, "Absolutely."

Soon after the merger, word got back to me that Doug wasn't happy with Jerry. When I asked Doug about it, he admitted he was losing patience with Jerry for working too slowly but hadn't talked to him about it. I said, "Doug, if anyone in your department needs to improve something, it's your fault until you tell them. They might be thinking they're doing a great job. You need to talk to Jerry." Next thing I know, I hear accusations that Jerry, who had been a drug user but had cleaned up his act, not only was stealing but was also using again. My new boss told me that even though he was sure that Jerry was innocent, it would be best for team morale if we let him go. That stung.

Unlike Jerry, who had been away from the company for years, my dad had consistently helped out in one capacity or another, but by the time of the merger he was working only ten to twenty hours a week. Being in the trenches like he was, my dad would hear a lot of company gossip, some of it about me, but he told me about it only if it was something serious I needed to know about, which wasn't often. Everyone at work treated my dad like he was their own dad or grandpa; his nickname was "Pa." He'd do anything for anyone there, from picking up parts to fixing mechanical problems. He'd even work on employees' cars if they asked him. One day, I heard rumblings about problems with my dad. The sources of the criticism appeared to be Russ in production and the guy in charge of the machine shop, who Kelly and Russ had apparently recruited for "Operation Zero Straitness." They were complaining that my dad was watching over everyone too closely and that people were afraid of him reporting every little snippet of gossip and breach of procedure to me. Just like when Jerry left the month before, it didn't matter that the claims were baseless. My new boss told me to let my dad go so we'd be in full compliance with the company's nepotism policy. Having to tell my father, "Sorry, you can't work here anymore," was one of the hardest things I ever had to do. Working there was so important to him. He was seventy years old and it gave him a place to go and something to do. It wasn't about the money, it was about the camaraderie. He was crushed that people he had considered family had sabotaged him.

With my father and brother banished, and a handful of key employees treating me like I was radioactive, it was not a happy time for me. I have to give Kelly credit—she knew how to carry out a clandestine mission. After my dad got forced out, I'm sure she celebrated: *Two Streitzes down, one to go. The last one's going to be a little tougher but I'll get him too.* That's not just a guess on my part. Much later, I heard that she boasted that she had gotten rid of Jerry and my dad. It made sense. She and her cronies could do more damage when I was out of town if my dad and brother weren't around to get in their way.

It was a phone call from the corporate office that opened the first fissure in Kelly's conspiracy. It seems that a few of my employees had called the Human Resources department to report that something weird was going on in Sauk Centre. So the HR Director called me and asked what was going on. On one hand, I was glad to get some support and validation; on the other hand, I wasn't happy that my bosses might be thinking that I wasn't in control of my own company. When you get acquired by a larger organization, the last thing you want to do is hit their radar because of a problem. Reluctantly, I told her that I had heard rumors that Kelly was trying to undermine me, although I hadn't reported it because I didn't have any proof. She agreed that it wasn't wise to fire anyone without hard evidence, and just asked me to keep my antennae up and keep her posted.

Soon after that call, I was getting set to leave on a business trip. There were some big projects in the works so I sent out a detailed e-mail to everyone involved that laid out everything that needed to happen while I was gone. The next day, I called a meeting to go over everything on the list to make sure everyone was on the same page. I also wanted to address the mounting tension I felt in the office, not realizing that the source of it was my gut feeling that Kelly was obsessed with overthrowing me. I stressed the importance of staying positive and professional, and encouraged anyone and everyone to come to me with any questions, disagreements, or ideas. Everyone in the room said they had complete clarity about everything we went over and assured me that I had nothing to worry about. I thanked everyone and headed out to the parking lot.

I was barely out of town when Cindy, my secretary, called to tell me that Kelly had just pulled everyone together, told them she was in charge while I was gone, and that they needed to do things her way instead of what we had all just agreed upon. I said, "You've got to be kidding." She said, "Nope." I told her to reschedule my flight, then turned around and drove back to the office. I walked in and headed straight for Kelly's office. "What happened?" I asked her. Looking confused, she said, "What do you mean, what happened?" I said, "I understand that you did exactly the opposite of what I requested. She looked me in the eye and said, "I didn't do that." Later that day, I tracked down the e-mail she had sent out right after I had left, so I called her into my office again, showed her the e-mail and took a softer approach. "What's going on, Kelly?" I said. "You know I think highly of you. You're a smart person. Why would you do this?" Knowing she was cornered, she played the "Woe is me" card and acted like a helpless victim. "I don't know, Paul," she said, looking crestfallen. "I just have so much stress in my life. You're a good man and I'm sorry I let you down. Please forgive me. It won't happen again." I told her I was going to hold her to that promise and said, "We can't have this happening, Kelly. It's not professional, and you know that." I left on my trip later that day, thankful that if Kelly was engaging in some sort of chicanery, I finally had some evidence to back up my suspicions.

It's always been my belief that bad seeds will end up burying themselves if you give them enough time. Sure enough, more evidence piled up while I was out of town that proved that my hunches about Kelly were well-founded. Before I returned to Minnesota, I was briefed on what had been discovered. The news hit me hard. Yes, I felt badly about being betrayed, but hearing the details only confirmed what I had already concluded myself. What also threw me was the gut-level realization that someone else was in more control of my company than I was. I had processed that information intellectually but it wasn't until now that it broke my heart.

Yes, I did feel betrayed. I had confided in Kelly. I had given her time off and bought her airline tickets when she needed to attend to personal matters. Apparently, Kelly viewed my kindness as a weakness to be exploited. That was hurtful, but what really tore me up was realizing that people I had known and trusted for years had believed her lies. I view myself as a positive, loving, honorable person and it was hard to accept that people who I thought were my friends believed I was capable of acting like an egomaniacal jerk.

The day after I returned from my trip, the phone rang at four in the morning. It was my new boss. He said, "Paul, you need to go to the AmericInn in Sauk Centre. Kathy, our representative, is there. Pick her up, have breakfast, you're going to fire Kelly Jones today." I said, "Really? Okay." Sleep-deprived and jet-lagged, I splashed some water on my face and drove over to pick up Kathy. At breakfast, I was shown Kelly's walking papers that the attorneys had prepared, documenting what company rules she had broken and so on and so forth. Kathy said, "You have to do the firing, Paul, but I'll be there in the room with you. All you have to say is, 'You're terminated, Kelly. Kathy's going to go over the paperwork with you.'"

As soon as Kathy and I arrived at the office, we got situated in a conference room, then called Kelly in. The moment I delivered the news to her, Kelly transformed into a woman possessed. Her face reddened, her nostrils flared, and I wouldn't have been surprised if she had started spitting fire. Kathy gave me a swift kick under the table as if to say, "Get the hell out of here, I'll take it from here." I didn't need to be told twice. Fifteen minutes later, Kelly stormed out, packed up her belongings, and headed for the door. Not surprisingly, she didn't go quietly. She was shouting insults until the door slammed behind her: "The Streitzes are the worst people in the world! They'll bring this company down!" I actually felt sorry for her.

I immediately called a staff meeting and briefed them on what had happened. I could see the relief on many of their faces. I said, "Listen, you guys, Kelly's gone, but we wish her the best." After the meeting, a couple employees who had never bought what Kelly was selling asked me why I had been so charitable to her after she had bad-mouthed me so viciously. I said, "Hey, it was just words. I'm comfortable with who I am and I don't wish anyone ill. What's important is that she's no longer part of our organization, so let's just worry about what we're going to do tomorrow."

Over the next few days, I searched through our company's computer system for e-mails in case Kelly decided to sue us for wrongful termination. Sifting through her e-mails was an eye-opening experience. There were dozens of instances of her e-mailing brazen lies and inflammatory accusations to the employees she was trying to win over to the dark side. If I had been aware of the extent of her treachery, I would have terminated her immediately.

It's true that the most important lessons are often the most painful to learn. I see now that I should have sent Kelly packing at the first inkling of disloyalty, hard evidence or not. If a cancer isn't cut out immediately, it will spread more quickly than you can imagine. If someone is radiating negative energy, it's the rest of your team that needs your caring, not just the person who's doing the damage.

One bad apple can rot the whole tree faster than you can say, "But I'm a nice guy; how could this happen?" I was contributing to poor morale by not trusting my instincts and naively thinking I could redeem the unredeemable.

Now that Kelly was history, I spent a lot of one-on-one time with the employees who had thrown in with her. We had some good heart-to-heart discussions and I feel like I won them back over. I knew things were going to be okay when Doug, the electronics manager, pulled me aside and said, "You know, she almost had me convinced that you were a bad guy, Paul. And I apologize for that." Doug was a good man who owned up to his mistakes. He handled things professionally, man to man, and I respected him for that.

Even though my employee relationships were repairable, something inside me had changed, which really bothered me. I had always believed that every individual, at their core, is a good person and that any problems could be fixed with love, compassion, and heartfelt communication. I still believe that Kelly was a decent person at heart, but her distorted worldview and lust for power eclipsed the goodness in her. After such a wrenching experience, I don't know that I'll ever be able to hire or work with somebody at that capacity without wondering about the limits of their integrity. Clearly, in Kelly's mind, the world was a dark and unfriendly place and she was content to live amidst the shadows, far beyond the reach of anyone's best intentions.

Power Play
Your Life, Your Thoughts

- Why is it dangerous to give too much weight to your gut feeling when hiring someone?

- What safeguards could be built into the hiring process to protect against hiring rabble-rousers?

- How diligent are you about documenting troubling incidents that would prove useful in a wrongful termination suit?

- How can you make it easier for employees to anonymously submit concerns and report problems?

- At what point should you stop giving troublemakers the benefit of the doubt and instead start doubting the benefit of retaining them?

- What are the pros and cons of having family members on the payroll?

- Why shouldn't you let someone who took advantage of your kindness and generosity stop you from being kind and generous to everyone else?

BURDENS AND BLESSINGS

At forty-three, with my life out of balance, I had a life-changing epiphany: If I was ever going to get married and start a family, I'd have to divorce my business. It was one or the other. I was married to the lighting company I had founded and it was running, and ruining, my life. Even during my rare vacations, work was all I thought about.

I felt like DeeDee, my girlfriend of six months, was "the one" and I didn't want to mess things up again. In all my previous relationships, I had devoted too much of my attention and energy to my career. I knew I was running out of time; the nagging voice in my head that told me I had missed out on something important was getting louder. I was convinced that if I couldn't separate my work life from my personal life, I would be a horrible husband and father and no woman would want to stay with me.

With all that on my mind, I almost fell to my knees in gratitude when a major competitor called a month later to ask if I'd be interested in merging my business into their publicly traded company. My prayers had been answered: Even though Advanced Lighting was "my baby," it was time to shrug off the burden and responsibility of running a business and get on with the business of living.

Four months later, the letter of intent to merge our companies became public knowledge. But I quickly found out that merging with a public company was like getting stung by hundreds of bees all day every day. Imagine being audited by the IRS, except instead of one agent looking over your records for a week, you had five of them literally moving in for six months and questioning you relentlessly about every last transaction over the last fourteen years. Seriously. They asked things like: "Why didn't you use your middle initial when you signed this form at the time you started the company but you did use your middle initial later on?"

Even though the merger process was taking a major toll on me, my relationship with DeeDee was holding up pretty well under the strain. I was more unavailable than usual, both physically and emotionally, but I knew things would be different once I could put the merger ordeal behind me. So in late July 2007 I made plans for us to fly to L.A. on a romantic vacation in late August, right after the scheduled closing date. I was super excited because I was going to ask DeeDee to marry me. Finally, my dreams would be coming full circle and my life would have more meaning.

That was the plan anyway. A week before the vacation, I got a call from my lawyers telling me the closing would be delayed up to six weeks due to some SEC (U.S. Securities and Exchange Commission) issues. I was devastated. Not because my huge payday was postponed but because I just wasn't comfortable proposing until I was officially a free man.

I was so bummed out and stressed out that we ended up having a miserable vacation. It didn't help that we were interrupted several times by calls from lawyers and accountants. We got along so poorly that I took it as a sign that we shouldn't get married. A week after we got back home—on my birthday, no less—I broke up with DeeDee, although we remained very friendly and continued to talk fairly often. Weeks later, as my closing date neared, I felt an oncoming sense of freedom and began feeling open to a possible reconciliation. When I told DeeDee I'd really like her to be with me in Minneapolis for the closing, she said she might be able to make it even though Minneapolis was a three-hour drive for her.

On the day of the closing I kept checking my phone for calls and text messages from DeeDee but saw nothing but a blank screen staring back at me. When the time came for me to sign the deal in the lawyers' office, my emotions were bouncing around like a pinball machine. On one hand, I was about to become a millionaire. On the other hand, I felt more alone than I ever had because not only didn't

I have a girlfriend anymore, I was about to lose my business too.

The papers were signed, the money was wired into my account, and I trudged back to my hotel room. A few minutes later, there was a knock on the door. I just knew it was DeeDee. I was all nervous and excited but when I opened the door my heart sank. There stood a hotel bellman delivering a bouquet of flowers. Okay, I thought, she couldn't come but at least she let me know she was thinking of me.

Then I looked at the card. It was from Tom Gegax, my business mentor and friend. Devastated all over again, I collapsed on my bed and sobbed for half an hour. On top of my crushing disappointment, I felt incredibly guilty: Tom had been so thoughtful and generous to send me a congratulatory bouquet but all I could think was *I wanted them to be from her.*

Finally, I collected myself and went down to the street to smoke a cigarette. It was a busy Minneapolis afternoon but every person and every car I saw seemed to be in slow motion. I just couldn't shake my funk. Suddenly, the phone rang. My heart leapt again, hoping it was DeeDee telling me she was on her way.

Nope. It was my mom, wondering if the closing had gone well. I told her that it had. Just from hearing me say those few words, she knew something wasn't right. When I told her what had happened, she told me that ever since I was a little boy she knew I was special. She said I always touched people in a positive way and that all their friends and relatives knew there was something exceptional about me and that I would do something incredible with my life. I was in tears. In a difficult moment, my mom made me realize that something really great had just happened and that I should be proud of myself for being a good person who was deserving of success.

Like a flash of lightning, it hit me that selling my business and having a few million bucks in the bank wouldn't automatically solve my problems after all. If I didn't have anyone to share it with, if I had no one to hold and no place to go, I'd just feel empty inside. What was I supposed to do, sit on my couch with a sack full of money and watch TV all day?

Walking away from my business so I could have a personal life had seemed logical at the time, but now I realized that I hadn't thought things through very well. I could have had both if I had just learned how to handle things differently. It hadn't been the business that was the problem after all, it was me.

I also realized that I couldn't imagine a life without work. But I knew that if and when I started a new business, the same problems would crop up again if I didn't figure out now how to keep my life in balance. Right then and there, I vowed not to let business consume my personal life ever again. I'm happy to say that I've kept my word.

Burdens And Blessings
Your Life, Your Thoughts

- If your professional life is compromising the quality of your personal life, what steps can you take to achieve a healthier balance between the two?

- What are three things you can do this week to begin improving the quality of the relationships that mean the most to you?

- Why is it misguided to look for meaning and purpose only from external sources?

- Why is it a mistake to expect financial security to make your life happier and more fulfilling?

- When you feel down and out, how can you remember to remind yourself that you are loved and cared for and have much to be grateful for?

SECTION II

SCHOOL'S IN SESSION

I didn't go to college but that's all right.
My on-the-job training in the Real World School
of Business earned me a double major
in Psychology and Character Building.

BALANCING THE BOOKS

I was visiting a client in Detroit one afternoon when I got a call that no small-business owner wants to get. It was from Cindy, my receptionist. "Oh, my God, everybody's going crazy," she said, her voice rising. "Everybody's paychecks are bouncing. They're all walking off the job." For a moment, I felt like I was high on drugs; I couldn't make any sense out of what she was saying. I managed to stammer, "What? You're kidding, right?" She blurted, "No, everybody's leaving!" I felt dizzy. I knew we had plenty of cash because I had just checked our balance prior to my trip. I hung up with Cindy, apologized to my client, cut my trip short, and took the next flight home.

On the plane back, the panic welling up in my chest made for a very unpleasant ride. Since banks don't usually make huge mistakes, I figured I must have screwed up but had no idea how. I also felt bad for my employees because many of them were living paycheck to paycheck. At the same time, I couldn't believe that people I had known and trusted for years would walk out on me without giving me the benefit of the doubt. I was as hurt as I was confused. Even worse, I felt utterly alone, a feeling I'm sure other small-business owners can relate to.

It was a sleepless night. When I got to work the next morning, there were enough cars in the parking lot to tell me that it was business as usual. I walked in, bracing myself for a barrage of questions; the last thing I expected to see was that everything would look so normal. But there was Cindy, answering the phones and Susan, the bookkeeper I had hired six months before, working quietly at her desk.

I looked at Cindy and said, "So . . . what's going on?" She looked at me, shrugged, and said, "I don't know," as innocently as she could. I glanced at Susan and got the same puzzled look back. I turned around, walked out the front door, and went straight to the bank, only to find out that no one's paycheck had bounced. What happened was that one of my employees had tried cashing her check there and, since our corporate account was also there, she was told there weren't enough funds to cash the check. But everybody else's check got cashed because the other employees who banked there had gotten there first. She came back to work and told everyone, "I can't believe it, my check didn't cash!" which, of course, got everybody up in arms. She was the only no-show that morning because her boyfriend told her I must be a crook and ordered her to stay home. When I got back from the bank, I called her and said, "Listen, there are funds in the account and you can cash your check. I'm sorry for the one-day delay, but something went wrong and I'm going to get to the bottom of it."

That night, after Susan went home, I sat at the computer and pored over the last three months' worth of books. All the checks looked legit, but after an hour or so I noticed that we had paid the phone company twice the previous month. The electric bill too. Bingo. I scrolled back and saw that the same thing had happened the month before and the month before that. I flagged those check numbers and kept searching, although I didn't really know what I was looking for. Whenever a vendor payment caught my eye for some reason, I flagged it. If an unfamiliar payee name jumped out at me, I added it to the list. By the time I finally switched off the computer, it was past midnight. I was so antsy, I hardly slept again that night. I was sure I was getting ripped off but I didn't have any proof. That would have to wait until the morning.

Instead of going into work the next day, I went straight to the bank. I gave my banker the list of suspect check numbers and waited while he looked them up and collected them for me. Back at the office, I compared the payees on the actual checks to the vendor names that had been entered on the computer. Yep, most of the checks were made out to different entities. It didn't take a brain surgeon to figure out that Susan had been using company funds to pay her personal bills. The largest bogus check each month—around $700—was made out to a company name I didn't recognize. I looked up their phone number and gave them a call. Turns out it was a timeshare in Mexico. When I said I was calling from Advanced Lighting, the guy who answered the phone assumed I was Susan's husband and said, "Oh, yes, Mr. Adams, we received your last payment from your wife's employer." I needn't have worried the night before about getting to the bottom of this mess. I now had all the proof I needed.

I had to give Susan credit. She was smart. The only reason I caught on to her scheme was because we were going through a lean time and our balance dipped a bit too low. I organized all the fraudulent checks, which added up to about eight grand, and without saying a word to anyone, left on foot for the police station. I sat down with an officer, showed him the evidence, and asked, "What are my options?" He said, "Well, we can go over right now and arrest her. You've got solid evidence that she's forging your name. In cases like this, normally what happens is you won't ever get restitution, but you'll get the satisfaction of sending her to jail." The only satisfaction I wanted was getting my money back so I asked what my other options were. He said, "Well, you can sue her, but if she's taking money from you, she probably has no money." I thanked the officer for his help and walked back to work.

I shut the door to my office, sat back, and did some thinking. I knew that Susan had recently gone through a divorce, had a young kid, and was struggling to get by. Stealing from me was inexcusable, but just like it hadn't done anybody any good to lock up my former girlfriend, Liliana, for accepting government assistance checks while she was working (see the "Loving Liliana" chapter for the full story), carting Susan off to jail wouldn't fix anything. It would only set her back even further and deprive her child of a mother. So I decided to give Susan a chance to do the right thing and get her life back on track.

The next morning, I called Susan into my office. She sat down across from me and a colleague who had agreed to serve as a witness. I handed her a letter and asked her to read it. As she did, her eyes grew wide and her breathing got shallow. The letter was actually an agreement, written from her perspective, that stated that she admitted to and accepted full responsibility for embezzling more than $8,000. Every forged check was listed. The agreement called for her to pay me $200 every week until the stolen amount was paid in full. When she finished reading it, she was on the verge of tears. I told her, "Either sign this letter or I pick up the phone and call the police, in which case you'll be prosecuted for a felony and probably go to jail." Trying to keep herself together, she flirtatiously said, "Isn't there some other way we can work this out?" I looked at her sternly and shook my head. Still looking hopeful, she said, "So, I'm not fired?" I said, "Oh, no. You're fired." She said, "Well, how am I going to pay you if I don't have a job?" I said, "You know what? That's not my problem. You stole from me and created a huge problem that forced me to come back early from a business trip and disappoint my customer. Your scheme cost me way more than what the checks added up to. I had to pay cancellation charges on my hotel and car rental, not to mention the bad morale you caused here and the stress and worry you caused me. I suggest you sit down with your family and find a way to make these payments."

Before handing her a pen, I said, "If there are any bad checks I missed, you better tell me right now. Because if I find even one more, this agreement is null and void and I'm going straight to the police." She looked over the list one more time and assured me that every forged check was accounted for. I also insisted that she personally come to my office every week and hand me a cashier's check or money order. That wasn't for my benefit, because, trust me, I didn't care to see her. I figured that delivering each check in person would remind her of the harm she had done. I also wanted her to see us grow and thrive as a company to drive home the point that unethical behavior comes at a steep cost.

Before concluding the meeting, I made Susan a promise and asked for one in return. I said, "As long as you fulfill your obligation, you have my word that I will not tell anyone outside of this company why you left. Furthermore, you're not to say a bad word about me either." She agreed, signed the agreement, went back to her desk to gather her things, and left.

I immediately called a team meeting to let everyone know what had happened. We had such a small company and lived in such a small town that I knew the word would get out and I wanted it handled the right way. I told everyone, "Look, I can't force you to say or not say anything, but the best thing to do is to keep this quiet, not only out of respect for Susan as a human being, but because we need her to find employment so she can pay us back."

I also called the meeting because there was much more at stake than the $8,000 that Susan had stolen. After the near-mutiny that Cindy had described to me over the phone, I knew I needed to shore up the relationship I had with my employees. I told them I had been really hurt that they had considered walking out because one person's paycheck didn't cash. When I asked why they had felt that way, they essentially said that I was a big city kind of guy who was always on the go and they didn't know what was going on. I told them I wasn't keeping any secrets from them and encouraged them to ask me anything they wanted at any time. I said, "Listen, you guys have been with me for a long time. Have you ever missed a paycheck?" They shook their heads. "Have I ever done anything to make you think you're not getting a paycheck?" More head shaking. I said, "So why would this time be any different just because I was out of town? When I'm gone on a trip, I trust you guys to do what you're getting paid to do, and I'm asking you to trust that I'm doing what I'm supposed to do." I told them that they were the core of the company and that they were always paid before anything or anybody else. I explained that the company was doing well and that the only reason why the check problem happened is because I was taken advantage of, which meant that they were taken advantage of too. I ended the meeting by saying, "In the future, if something comes up, I'd appreciate it if you'd come talk to me before jumping to any conclusions." From then on, I made it a point to hold monthly employee meetings to keep everyone more informed and engaged. Ultimately, even though their lack of faith in me was disheartening, Susan's embezzling provided an opportunity for me to get closer to my employees and help us understand each other.

Five days after she was fired, Susan showed up with her first payment. To her credit, she came in like clockwork every week after that. She was never an hour late or a dollar short. From time to time, I'd see her around town. She was working as a waitress at a local café and had a second job too. To my knowledge, she never said a bad word about me in the community. In fact, through the rumor mill, I heard she was telling people that I had a big heart and was a great guy to work for. I kept my end of the bargain too. When anyone asked about her, I said she had done a good job but it just didn't work out and I wished her the best. Yes, some of her former coworkers couldn't resist gossiping about her but I think that was kept pretty well in check.

I remember the day of Susan's final payment. She came in looking very happy and excited. She handed me the cashier's check and thanked me again for not pressing charges and giving her a chance to make things right. I said, "Susan, I'm proud of you for owning up to your mistakes and taking responsibility." Before she left, she apologized again for what she had done and I could feel her sincerity. I was glad to see that she had treated this second chance as a wake-up call and had turned her life around. In the end, everybody won: I got my money back, Susan learned a valuable life lesson, and I strengthened my relationship with my employees along the way.

Balancing The Books
Your Life, Your Thoughts

- When was the last time you felt panicked at work about a situation that came out of nowhere?

- What safeguards do you have in place to prevent, or at least minimize, employee theft?

- What are three things you can do right now to deepen the trust and rapport you have with your employees?

- What are some challenges you've had that may have turned out better had you applied a win-win approach?

WHATEVER IT TAKES

Five years and three moves after teaming up with my brother Jerry at Advanced Lighting, the company had grown so much that I built a big new manufacturing facility. It was a proud moment, considering that Advanced Lighting had started from scratch in the basement of a chiropractor's office. I was super excited to move in, so as soon as the new building was finished I made plans to shut down operations in our current location that Friday and get everything moved into the new facility over the weekend. If all went well, we'd and be up and running again Monday morning.

Luckily, Paul, a local guy I knew who owned a large excavation company, said I could use his 18-wheeler semi for the move. Paul drove the semi over to the warehouse I had been renting, backed it up to the loading dock, handed me the keys, and said, "After you load it, call me and I'll drive it over to your new place so you can unload it. We'll just keep doing that until you're done." He then hopped into the truck of an employee who had followed him there to give him a ride back to his office.

As we were wrapping up the first load, I called Paul but there was no answer. I waited five minutes and called again. Still no luck. I kept trying every few minutes until he finally answered. "I'm busy," he said. "Just drive it yourself." And he hung up. I looked around at everybody and said, "Does anybody know how to drive a semi truck?" Nobody did.

I racked my brain trying to think of somebody I knew who might have a license to drive a semi but drew a blank. Then something came over me and I thought, *Screw it! This has gotta get done.* My customers didn't want to hear that their orders would be late because all our equipment was on a truck that no one knew how to drive.

I figured, *What the hell, I can drive a stick shift,* so I jumped in the cab and took the wheel. I pulled out and started driving down the road, thinking, *Hey, this isn't so bad.* Then I reached our new industrial park and thought, *Oh, crap!* I had to back that bad boy into a loading dock from the street. That meant I had to make a sharp turn, straighten the whole thing out, and back it all the way up until I was perfectly lined up with the loading dock. It took me a few tries just to straighten the truck, and the cars I was blocking on the main road let me know they weren't too pleased about waiting. As I backed up toward the loading dock, I started to breathe a little easier; it looked like this was going to work after all.

Just a few more feet and . . . *crap! I* was stuck in the mud! It had been a long winter and the snow was melting, so the parking lot was nothing but soupy, muddy dirt. I gunned the engine but couldn't gain any traction; I just kept spinning the tires. When I rocked the truck back and forth like it was a car stuck in a snow drift, it finally came unstuck and rammed into the loading dock. It wasn't lined up just right but it was close enough. After we unloaded the truck, I drove back to the loading dock at our old building for another load. By the fifth load, I was getting the hang of making sharp turns and backing up. We got all six loads moved in and we were up and running Monday morning.

I never thought I'd find myself behind the wheel of a semi, but when the job needs to get done, you do whatever it takes. It never entered my mind that I wouldn't be able to drive that truck. Yes, driving a semi without a license was illegal but it was a risk worth taking in order to keep my business going and honor my commitments to my customers. When you're out of options and your business is on the line, it's amazing what you can do.

A perfect storm of circumstances put me in another do-or-die position a few years later. It was Friday afternoon and I had just returned to Minneapolis from an overseas business trip. I headed for the nearest taxi because my car was waiting for me at a dealership not far from the airport. Since I live two hours from Minneapolis, I made a habit of dropping my car off to get serviced whenever I flew out of town; that way, my car would be fixed and waiting for me and I wouldn't have to pay for parking while I was gone.

My flight had touched down at four-thirty and I needed to get to the dealership by the time they closed at six. Usually, that would be no problem but a major snowstorm had just moved in and traffic was backed up. The taxi driver loaded my bags in the trunk and off we went. As soon as we left the sheltered taxi area and hit the freeway, it was obvious that my driver, a Somalian, had never driven in a snowstorm. He was super nervous and mumbling what must have been a prayer in his native language. He was gripping the steering wheel so hard he almost ground it into powder.

We were inching along on the freeway at five miles an hour while everyone else was zipping by us. I said, "Are you all right?" He was so petrified that he just muttered something unintelligible. I asked him to drive a bit faster but as soon as he picked up his speed, we did a 360, spinning completely around. It's a miracle nobody slammed into us. Before my heart even stopped racing, he sideswiped the brick divider in the center of the highway. That did it. At the rate we were going, we'd never make it to the dealership in one piece, much less before it closed. And if I couldn't get my car, I'd be stranded in Minneapolis for the weekend. There was only one thing to do: I shouted at him to pull over. I got out of the car, walked around to the driver's side door, opened it, and said, "Get out. Get in the back seat." He looked stunned, but also relieved, like he wanted to say, *You can't do this . . . Oh, God, thank you!*

So there I was, all dressed up in business attire, driving a taxicab down the freeway in a snowstorm. I'm a native Minnesotan, so driving in snow was no big deal. I was trucking along at thirty miles per hour with the rest of the traffic and glancing at my watch. I was making good progress, but a few minutes before 6:00 I was more than ten minutes away. I pulled out my phone, turned off the freeway and started booking down every back road I could take. The guy at the dealership was great, assuring me that he'd stay open until I got there. I gave him my credit card info so he'd have everything ready for me to sign. I pulled into the lot about eight minutes after six, told the taxi driver I'd be right back, and ran into the service bay. I took care of the paperwork, pulled my car out, and got out to pay the taxi guy, who still seemed scared out of his mind. He looked up at me with a "What do I do now?" expression. I just shrugged and told him to wait out the storm. A few hours later I was home.

How many people would have taken the wheel of that cab like I did? Probably not many. Most would have toughed it out in the back seat, not gotten to their car in time, and ended up in a hotel until Monday morning. I refused to consider that option. I don't believe in accepting things the way they are if the way they are isn't good enough. There's always another way. There's always something you can do.

Whatever It Takes
Your Life, Your Thoughts

- What experience comes to mind when you think of a time you blew past your self-imposed limitations and surprised yourself with what you were capable of?

- What goes through your mind when you come up against a seemingly insurmountable roadblock that threatens your ability to complete an important mission or project?

- Looking back on scenarios in which you threw up your hands and thought, There's nothing I can do, what could you have done differently by thinking more creatively and refusing to give up?

NO EXCUSES

Advanced Lighting was the get-it-done company. We became successful because we delivered products that were built right and on time. If you're scratching your head and thinking that doing what you said you were going to do should be a given instead of a competitive advantage, I'm with you. But in the entertainment industry, most of our competitors were either inefficient, incompetent, or incapable of producing the kind of quality products we specialized in. Honoring our commitments was more than just a good business practice, it was a matter of personal integrity.

Our closest call to missing a deadline was for a fiber optic curtain for the Country Tonite Theater in Pigeon Forge, Tennessee. The curtain was going to be the major backdrop for a new show and we were running behind. The show opened on Friday and the glue finally dried on Thursday. Once we got the curtain packed up, it was too big to air freight, and sending it by truck wouldn't get it there on time. My dad and I looked at each other, and without a word we knew what we had to do. We rented a big cargo van, loaded up the curtain, and hit the road around 7 PM. Eighteen hours later, after winding through the mountains of Tennessee, we pulled up at the theater, helped install the curtain, and left as heroes.

Did I have options? Sure, if you consider not keeping your word an option. We could have double-talked our way into a delay by blaming the wait on other vendors, on technicalities, or even on the customer themselves. I'm sure we could have gotten away with that but we would've never seen another order from them. On top of that, show business production folks typically jump from project to project and theater to theater. If we hadn't shown up on time and the show had to be canceled, that news would have gone viral and our market share in that entertainment hotbed would have plummeted. Instead, we drove all night to deliver the curtain on time. Did the customer know that? Nope. They just thought we had great customer service. Ultimately, in show business you have no choice; you have to show up because the show must go on.

Our decision to compete on service came down to a two-word mantra: *No excuses.* It doesn't matter how tired you are, how sick you might be, or if your personal life is in upheaval. You have to do whatever it takes—whether that means pitching in on the production floor, getting your hands dirty in shipping, or driving cross-country—to get the job done.

Once you make that commitment to be all in, your mind becomes clear to focus on solutions instead of excuses, and you end up getting a euphoric high from accomplishing the impossible. The second you start making excuses, you might as well lock your doors and shut your business down because someone else is going to come along who's hungrier than you are.

In 2002, the year after we drove all night to Pigeon Forge, we bid on a big fiber optic curtain project for Britney Spears' tour. We wanted to get it because featuring her name on our client list would open even more doors for us. Unfortunately, Jack, who was in charge of Britney's production team, selected FiberFan, one of our competitors. Three weeks later, on a Monday morning, I got a call from Jack. "I just checked in with the people we gave the order to," he said, sounding desperate. "They're running a week behind and the show starts this Friday." When I asked Jack how I could help, he asked if I could make the curtain. I said, "Well, I've got all the materials but we're super-busy. Let me see if I can reprioritize any of the projects I have on the floor that have some extra time built in." I huddled with my floor manager and we determined that we could move some things around and squeeze in the job, but that it still would take some serious miracle-making on our part to get the curtain finished and on a plane in only three days.

I called Jack back and said, "Listen, here's the deal. We'll get it done. I've got a dedicated crew that's willing to work all night if they have to. But this thing might show up literally an hour before the concert on Friday." I could hear him breathe a big sigh of relief. When I told him I wouldn't charge him a penny more than our original bid, he protested and said he was ready to write a bigger check. I said, "No, that's not necessary. What I want is your business in the future. I don't want you to even consider another company." Without hesitation, Jack said, "No problem, you got it."

Immediately, we cleared production space and got to work. For the next three days, it was all Britney Spears all the time. We finished the curtain on Thursday morning, packed it up, and couriered it to the airport. Jack had it that night, twenty-four hours before the concert. He called me in shock and said, "How could you build this in three days when your competitor couldn't do it in four weeks?" I said, "There's more than one way to make things happen. It doesn't take that long to build, but it takes a lot of organization to do multiple projects at once and do right by all our customers." Jack thanked me profusely, and I said, "Look, it's not your fault that FiberFan is running late. I don't want you to wear egg on your face in front of your clients. What was most important was to make sure this concert happens." Jack was true to his word and gave us a ton of business going forward.

That type of scenario was not uncommon. We got a lot of last-minute orders as word spread that we were the company to call when everyone else said no. Not only did we save the day for panicked customers, we often charged less than our competitors thanks to our location in a rural Minnesota town that gave us tax-increment financing to build a facility.

One reason we were able to be so flexible and accommodating is that our entire company was in one building while our major competitor's headquarters was in one facility with their manufacturing in another. That might work if you're a huge manufacturing firm, but not if you're in an entrepreneurial business. You need the entire team there working together, with everybody grabbing something and helping out if needed. Everyone at Advanced Lighting cared about getting things right and doing things right. Whether it was me, our controller, or a salesperson, someone was always walking the shop floor lending a helping hand or double-checking packaging and shipping specs. Our goal was to establish such high standards of performance and trust that our customers would have no reason to look anywhere else.

We grew even more successful when we branched into other markets. Custom manufacturers who built LED fixtures for the architectural market typically demanded a minimum of four weeks for jobs and often told frantic customers who called on the due date that they'd have to wait another week or two. That's not how we did business. If a building was framed in and ready for custom fixtures to be hung, our being late could cost a union crew thousands of dollars. As architectural firms learned that we always kept our word, our receptionist couldn't answer the phone fast enough.

Over time, our hard-earned reputation for guaranteed quality, on-time delivery, and low cost made us the go-to choice for any and all fiber optic and LED lighting products. Our value proposition was so unique that after I sold the business, I got a call from a former customer who urged me to jump back in the fiber optic and LED business. He said, "I'll open up the business for you and guarantee you so much per month if you just start another company so I can buy from you again." I thanked him but explained that I intended to honor my non-compete clause. Still, it felt good to get the offer, and it drove home the point that top-tier customers will always demand the very best quality and service and pay handsomely for the privilege.

No Excuses
Your Life, Your Thoughts

- How is the integrity of your business an extension of your personal integrity?

- What are three reasons why "I'm sorry, but . . ." is the most dangerous way to start a conversation with a customer?

- Why is satisfying your customer infinitely more important than the profit you make on their order?

- What is the secret to making the impossible possible?

- How can you enhance your reputation as the go-to place for superior quality and world-class service?

I DON'T KNOW

When life gives you a big enough target, it's easier to hit the bull's-eye. Sure enough, when we hooked up with Target Corporation in 2004, we wound up lighting up half of New York City. It all began with a voicemail: "Hi, this is Melissa. I'm in charge of print buying and special projects at Target. We have a project we'd like you to come down for. We were referred to you by Don Robertson from 3M." Hello! That made me sit up straight. A project involving both Target and 3M had to be huge, and it was especially cool that two multibillion-dollar companies would turn to a small entrepreneurial company in a podunk town like Sauk Centre.

I immediately called Don, who was in charge of fiber optic lighting for 3M. Don, who had done a lot of business with us, told me he had been consulting with Target on a project for the better part of a year before finally telling Melissa, "Listen, I don't know that we can do this. You need to call Paul Streitz at Advanced Lighting." Before hanging up with me, Don said, "This is your area of expertise, Paul. Run with it."

I called Melissa, introduced myself, and set up a time to get together. The morning of the meeting, I suited up and drove the hundred miles to Target's Minneapolis corporate headquarters. Melissa welcomed me into her office and explained that they wanted to create a billboard in Times Square that was lit with floodlights but that also included certain elements that lit up at nighttime and appeared animated. When she asked if fiber optics was the answer, I said, "I don't know. But I'll get right to work on it and build you a prototype." She asked how long that would take, and was thrilled when I said I'd have it done in a week. When I got back to my office, I attached some fiber optic lights in the shape of the Target logo to a piece of plywood. I painted it up nice and set up a program sequence to turn it on and off when it was plugged in. I called Melissa and told her we were good to go.

We had to wait a few weeks until all of Melissa's colleagues would be available for a meeting. When I arrived at the appointed time, she walked me into the conference room and introduced me to one high-ranking executive after another. I got right to business and demo'ed the prototype. Everyone loved it. They said, "It's great! It's bright and it disappears when it's not on. Can you do this in vinyl and put it on a billboard?" I said, "I don't know, but I don't see why not." Next thing I knew, people started firing questions at me about our capabilities and experience. It was a little surreal because I still was pretty clueless about the project details, although given that the conference room was chock-full of v.p.'s, it was obvious that something big was brewing. I explained that my company's primary focus was on entertainment and commercial lighting, but that billboards weren't much of a stretch considering that the hanging devices we created for Broadway shows were similar to billboards in that they both displayed images and messages.

At that point, Melissa showed me the artwork and renderings for what they had in mind and told me the scope of the job. Whoa. I had been under the impression we were talking about one billboard. Nope. They wanted to wrap *an entire square block* of Times Square in vinyl billboards for their Fourth of July summer campaign. That's 23,000 square feet of billboard space on the Port Authority building, probably the most trafficked area in Times Square. I thought, *Oh, my God, this is massive.* When Melissa asked if I could do it, I calmly said, "I don't know, but I'm willing to try." That was exactly the right thing to say. Target prides itself on being innovative and first to market, so they were excited that a leader in the fiber optic lighting industry had no knowledge of such an application. They correctly interpreted my saying "I don't know" as "I don't think anybody's done this yet." I learned later that this undertaking was a first on two fronts: Not only was Target pioneering fiber optic billboards, no one had done *any* type of billboard project of that magnitude without the use of giant props. I suggested to the execs that they rent me some billboard space off the freeway near our Sauk Centre factory so we could experiment and see if we could make the concept work.

Big, bold projects are always exciting, and working out the logistics was a blast. Positioning a bunch of fiber optic Target logos, shooting stars, bubbles, and other images on a 14' x 48' vinyl backdrop was the easy part. What we didn't know was how the billboard would hold up in bad weather or whether the combined weight of all the components would bring it all crashing down. We were also concerned that the billboard might look "lumpy." The images would be laying flat on the billboard but we'd be poking holes in them and gluing our fiber on the back side. Even though the fibers would stick out a bit on the front of the images, they'd be virtually invisible to the eye because a fiber optic cable is the size of a human hair. Complicating matters further, since we'd be using millions of feet of fiber optic cable, we'd be connecting thousands of fiber "tails" in back of the billboard to seven illuminators that were custom-programmed to light up and animate the images at night. In one area, for instance, the Target bull's-eye had to "pop out" of a dandelion when two children blew on it.

It took two weeks to put all the puzzle pieces together. As soon as we glued on the last fibers and double-checked everything, we called the billboard company to come pick it up. We followed them to the nearby freeway and spent two hours helping them hang it up. It looked good, just like a normal billboard; from the freeway, you couldn't tell there were tens of thousands of points of light and fiber mounted on the vinyl backdrop. Best of all, it didn't fall apart. The hardest part of the whole project was having to wait five hours for night to fall so we could see if it all lit up and moved like it was supposed to. I was so eager that it was pointless trying to concentrate on anything else. After all, if this worked, we'd get a massive project with fees to match. Finally, it got dark out. We hit the switch and . . . voilà! It looked awesome! I immediately called Melissa to give her the good news.

After three weeks of exposure to the elements, including heavy winds and rain, the billboard still looked great. Now that we had proven that the idea could work, Melissa asked if we were ready to go all out with the Times Square project. I told her, "Yes, we can mechanically do this. We can ship you the backdrops, you can hang them, and they should work. But I cannot guarantee them because the billboards you're proposing are more than twice the square footage of the standard-size board we did in Sauk Centre. I don't know if the fiber will hold up in transportation or whether the vinyl will rip during the hanging from the weight of all the components. But if you're willing to take the risk, we'll build them for you." Melissa didn't hesitate. "We'll take the chance," she said.

I sat down with a calculator and totaled up the project bid, which came out to more than half a million bucks. Melissa gave me the green light and we got to work. Four weeks later, 23,000 square feet of vinyl backdrops were loaded onto trucks and shipped to a New York billboard company. I flew out to New York to supervise the installation and my electronics guy joined me three days later. When all the billboards were up, Times Square looked like a giant Target store. That first night was magical; everything worked exactly as planned. I stuck around a few more days in case there were unforeseen complications, but everything was working so smoothly I decided to fly home. I was thrilled that everything had gone so well but I was still plenty worried; for all I knew, the billboards could collapse under their own weight at any moment.

When I walked back into my office in Sauk Centre, there was a voicemail from Melissa waiting for me. Instead of her usual cheerful tone, she was matter-of-fact and businesslike. "Hi, Paul. It's Melissa from Target. When you get in, we need to talk about those billboards." My heart dropped into my stomach and my mind flashed back to watching in horror as the *Ragtime* curtain self-destructed. I envisioned billboards ripping in half and millions of feet of fiber optic cable raining down on panicked pedestrians. My finger was almost trembling as I dialed Melissa's number. When she answered, she said, "Oh, hi, Paul. I wanted to talk about the next billboards we'd like you to do for our Christmas campaign and whether we can reuse the illuminators." I just about dropped to my knees in relief and gratitude. "You bet, "I told her. "Can't wait to get started!"

To this day, I'm convinced that those three magic words—"I don't know"—were the foundation for a great relationship with Target. I knew the technology would work, I just wasn't sure if the laws of physics would be on our side. That's why I kept coming back to "I don't know." Not only were we talking about unexplored territory, it was important for me to manage expectations. By acknowledging I didn't have all the answers, I eliminated my risk and avoided setting myself up as a failure had the project not worked. Instead, the prevailing attitude was, "Hey, we're all in this together. Let's give it a go and see if it works."

Even more importantly, saying "I don't know" went a long way toward earning the respect of Team Target. Whether in business or personal life, one thing I do know is that people tend to respect you even more when you're authentically transparent and humble, with no agenda other than giving your very best effort.

I Don't Know
Your Life, Your Thoughts

- What are three reasons why saying "I don't know" is the smart answer when you don't know the answer?

- What's the first thought that comes to mind when you imagine a customer asking you to stretch yourself far beyond the capacity of your largest project to date?

- What do you like and dislike about the challenge of going further than you've ever gone before?

- How can you do a better job of managing expectations on big projects?

- Why does genuine humility serve you better than bold promises?

LIVING WITHOUT LIMITS

The entrepreneurial flame has been burning in me for as long as I can remember. Looking back, I'm amazed I was able to keep it from flickering out, considering that so many people around me tried to smother it with their good intentions. It's a real head-scratcher that so many people think you'd be better off strangling your dreams at birth than taking even the smallest risk.

That's essentially what Margaret told me the whole time we were dating. It was 1993 and I was thinking of joining my brother, Jerry, at Advanced Lighting. She'd say things like, "Why don't you just fly and enjoy it? You make a good living, what's wrong with that?" I tried explaining to her that dreaming up business ideas wasn't something I decided to do one day, it was *who I was*. She was particularly incredulous when I told her I was thinking of getting back into lighting. "You got screwed by everybody in that business," she'd point out. I'd say, "Yeah, but this is different because this time I'll be in business with my brother. It's family and I'll have some ownership and control." I knew that Margaret wasn't intentionally putting me down; her vibe was, "Hey, why don't you just enjoy life instead of putting yourself through all that grief?" Still, I wasn't too upset when we decided to break up.

Margaret was a cheerleader compared to my Grandma Norma. Why is it that family members are often the most notorious dream-killers? Grandma Norma would tell me, "Paulie, you're a big dreamer. You've got a good union job, just stick to that." That didn't make much sense to me, considering that she and my step-grandpa had owned a successful trucking business. Even worse, my parents sang from the same songbook as Grandma Norma. They couldn't understand why I wanted to gamble with my future instead of playing it safe. It didn't make sense to them that I couldn't bear the thought of being a flight attendant for the rest of my life.

I have to admit that I let all that dreary "Why take a chance?" talk get to me at times. In fact, I still hear those voices in my head occasionally. None of the naysayers were deliberately being negative; somewhere along the way, they had let fear get the better of them. Instead of saying yes to life, they had weighed themselves down with the ball and chain of low expectations and limiting beliefs. They were more concerned with protection from disappointment than with experiencing the joy that life has to offer.

Fortunately, there was some force inside of me that urged me to seek out more positive thinkers and role models. My Uncle Curt was entrepreneurial and I hung out with him whenever I could, learning quite a bit about business. I was also lucky to meet some friends along the way who'd say, "You can do it, Paul. Go for it!" That kind of encouragement and support was great, but it was even more helpful when people shared practical tips and advice based on their own experiences. Shoring up my dreams with realistic plans and goals enabled me to have my head in the clouds and my feet on the ground at the same time.

I credit a big part of my success to associating with other successful people, especially those with an entrepreneurial mindset. The most valuable connection I made was with Tom Gegax, the founder of the Tires Plus chain of retail tire stores, whom I met in 2005. I hired Tom as my business mentor and life coach, and we subsequently became good friends. Tom opened my eyes to new and better ways of looking at the world. As I absorbed his knowledge and positive approach to life, I started changing for the better, although I didn't realize it at the time.

After I sold Advanced Lighting in 2007, Tom told me he was taking me to a celebration dinner at The Oceanaire Seafood Room, one of the most elegant restaurants in the Twin Cities. The maître d' put us on a wait list and we headed for the bar, where we struck up a conversation with a couple next to us who were out on a date. The girl and I hit it off and we had a great time until our table was ready. As

Tom and I left the bar, he said, "Did you see what just happened?" I looked at him blankly. "That girl was very into you," he said. "She was very engaging, she was twirling her hair; you really made an impression on her." I was shocked. "Oh, no I didn't," I protested. "Didn't you notice that her date was getting upset?" Tom asked with a twinkle in his eye. As I replayed the scene in my mind, it dawned on me that Tom was right. Had I known I was interfering in their date, I would have politely excused myself from the conversation.

Tom's impromptu feedback sparked some serious introspection. On some level, I knew I was holding on to a self-image that no longer served me, but it was a comfortable place to live and a convenient excuse whenever I wanted an easy way out. Essentially, I was still looking at myself the way I did when I was immature, insecure, and socially awkward—when I thought I'd always be a nobody.

Thanks to Tom's coaching and positive influence, I realized I had a lot more to offer than the old tapes playing in my head told me I did. I challenged myself to see the Paul that other people were seeing: the confident, intelligent, and likable Paul. Instead of thinking I was just an ordinary, uneducated guy with no credentials who lived in a small town in the middle of nowhere, I began telling myself I was a creative guy with great people skills and solid values who was fun to be around. Even though I could see the truth in that statement, it wasn't easy to rewrite those old tapes and reinvent myself. That's why, at Tom's urging, I started seeing Brenda Schaeffer, a well-known relationship therapist and best-selling author. Brenda helped me understand why I had been subtly sabotaging not only my romantic relationships but also my professional and personal lives. The common theme snaking through every issue in my life was the limiting assumption that I wasn't smart enough or capable enough to be truly successful and happy. After five months of working with Brenda, I finally saw that assumption for what it was: a smokescreen conjured up by my fears and insecurities that prevented me from realizing my full potential. I needed to set higher standards—first for myself, and then for the people I worked with and the women I dated. It was hard work but I loved it, and it felt awesome to reboot and launch Paul 2.0 into the world.

Now that I was more comfortable in my own skin, I started noticing that others started gravitating toward me at parties and other gatherings. When I talked to people, they were fully engaged in the conversation, listened intently, and valued what I had to say. The only thing that had changed was my perspective, and yet that changed everything. What a powerful realization: As soon as we believe in ourselves, other people will too.

I'll never forget the night that Tom hosted a fundraiser for Waterkeeper Alliance, the environmental organization founded by Bobby Kennedy, Jr. Tom's house was filled with business and cultural leaders from the Twin Cities area, from University of Minnesota men's basketball coach Tubby Smith to international explorer Will Steger. Attending that event was a big test for me, not only because I'd be mingling with all those heavy hitters but because of my physical appearance. I had decided to get a hair transplant long before my hair loss was noticeable, and my surgery happened to be the day before. I had half-inch long stubble all around my head; it was all red and flaky and disgusting. A year earlier, I never would have considered going in that condition; I would have been too insecure and self-conscious. But thanks to Tom's coaching and encouragement, I was now confident enough in who I was as a person to show up, warts and all, and not worry about what others might think. I'm so glad I felt secure enough to go, because I had an awesome time. If I had stayed home, I would have missed out on meeting incredible people like Bobby Kennedy, Jr. and enjoying lively conversations. In fact, I was told more than once that I was the life of the party! I found out later that I had left a lasting impression on people, not because of my hair transplant but for all the right reasons. Over the next few days, Tom told me he got messages from people saying things like, "Who was that Paul Streitz guy? I enjoyed getting to know him. He was really entertaining." Hearing those comments was both humbling and exciting: humbling because they were tangible reminders of how far I had come, and exciting because I felt like I had stepped into a whole new world of fascinating ideas, experiences, and people.

The Waterkeeper party was also a wake-up call for me to look past appearances to find the beauty in every individual. Just as the people at Tom's house were willing to see if the goofball with the stitches all over his head had something interesting to offer, I challenged myself to give the same consideration to others, to get past any initial judgments and find something great about them. I even turned it into a game. At every business event I attended, I would say to myself, "I'm going to try to find one thing that I admire about everyone I meet today." It was easier than I expected. All I had to do was give my full attention to people and ask questions like, "So what do you like about what you do?", "What would your dream job be?", and "What else are you really passionate about?" I was surprised at how quickly I could establish a connection with somebody and elevate a casual conversation into something more personal and meaningful. I took the same attitude with me to parties and other social get-togethers. Whereas the old me would have felt nervous and awkward in a room full of strangers, I now walked in thinking, *This is going to be fun! I bet I'm going to meet some cool people and learn some interesting things.* And I always did.

Even though I absolutely believe that every person is a buried treasure just waiting to be discovered, it's easy to fall into the trap of judging others based on first impressions. Visualizing myself talking to Bobby Kennedy, Jr. with a head full of red marks is a good reminder to practice humility and empathy. Recently, on a ten-hour flight back from Amsterdam, I was sitting in an aisle seat when an attractive young woman sat down next to me. She was quiet at first, and since I'm not a fan of long, awkward silences, I made a point to find out something about her. I soon found out that her name was Lisa and that she was a Minnesota native who was now living and working in Denmark in the IT business. As she was telling me about the guy she was dating, a heavyset, disheveled couple boarded and sat across the aisle from us. Both of them were white, but the three-month-old infant they had with them appeared to be African. As soon as they sat down, my seatmate and I grimaced and glanced at each other as if to say, "Do you smell that?" I mouthed to her, "Oh. My. God." Whatever it was, it reeked big time and we were directly in the line of fire.

Over the next couple of hours, whenever the guy across from me would shift in his seat, it was as if a Ziploc baggie broke its seal and an odor most foul wafted over us. Fortunately, Lisa was carrying some sort of body spray that she'd strategically deploy to counteract the fumes. Each time she sprayed it, we'd look at each other and giggle. The flight attendant, who was well aware of our plight, discreetly whispered to us that there were seats available in the back of the plane if we wanted to escape the smell. Lisa and I glanced at each other. We were enjoying each other's company, and besides, we were intrigued by the family across from us and just had to know their story. I said to the attendant, "You know what? We've got our little spray perfume and we're good. Thanks."

When the timing felt right, I turned toward the aisle and asked Mr. Malodorous where he was from. He said that he and his wife were from Rapid

City, South Dakota, and had just adopted a baby from Uganda. They had been required to stay in the country for three weeks to satisfy the adoption requirements. The more we spoke, the more I liked this couple. Here they had traveled to the other side of the world in order to give an orphaned child from another country loving parents and a chance for a great life. Even though I had suspected as much from the get-go, I still felt a bit guilty for poking fun at them. Once we learned their story, Lisa and I felt privileged to be sitting next to such selfless, beautiful people. Obviously, there was a good reason why they smelled bad: they had just spent three weeks in a third-world country with a week's worth of clothing and poor laundry options. They also had been traveling for eighteen hours by the time they boarded our plane. Hell, I would've stunk like sweaty gym socks too.

When I considered how close I had come to writing this couple off, I couldn't help but think back to a Miami-to-Madrid flight I had worked back in 1995. Those were the days when we welcomed people to first class with flower bouquets, fancy drinks, and specialty chocolates. As first class was filling up, in walked three or four guys who were dressed and groomed so shabbily that they could've passed for vagrants. They immediately drew disapproving looks from the other passengers; I even saw a few flight attendants in the galley sneaking looks and whispering about them. Next thing I knew, two security officers appeared and started questioning these guys. I was appalled, because I had recognized those passengers as soon as they boarded. They were members of the Gypsy Kings, a group of European musicians who are famous for their pop-oriented flamenco performances. I was a huge fan and still listen to their music. I walked over and told security, "Hey, guys, these are the Gypsy Kings; they're amazing artists and huge international stars." I apologized to the band members but they just smiled and said, "No problem, no problem." They couldn't have been more gracious. Later in the flight, I had a chance to talk to them. They acknowledged that because of the way they dress, which is in homage to their culture, they recognize that people in other parts of the world are going to judge them. Even so, I was embarrassed by the behavior of my colleagues, especially whoever it was who reported them to security. I hope that everyone on that flight who looked askance at the Gypsy Kings gained some insight into the pitfalls of condemning others on appearance alone.

I'm grateful I learned those lessons when I did. Training myself to see the best in every person and the beauty in every moment transformed every circumstance, every situation, and even every hardship into an opportunity for counting my blessings. In those rare moments when I do throw myself a pity party, all I have to do is look around at my beautiful home and the successful life I've been fortunate enough to build. Growing up, I never would have imagined that achieving all this was even a possibility. Appreciating what I do have always trumps moaning about what I don't have.

Having experienced the power of reframing, I love helping others shift their perspective too. Veronica, a friend of mind, tends to write negative, "woe is me" types of posts on Facebook. I'm careful not to be too preachy but I try to give her a nudge in the right direction whenever I can. For instance, here's the way one of her status updates looked: "Oh, God, it's Sunday night, I've gotta get up early, drive (25 miles) to St. Cloud, go to work, come home and eat dinner, take the dog for a walk, and then do it all over again." She had been unemployed for a while, so I commented, "That's fantastic! You've got a job. You've got a car. You're earning money. And you have a wonderful pet who's waiting to love you when you get home. What a great routine. That's awesome!" Her Debbie Downer response was, "Yeah, I suppose."

What Veronica doesn't understand is that the way she sees the world isn't the way the world absolutely is, it's only her perception of the world. When you hear people talk about "creating your own reality," that's what they mean. In my world, the days were mostly sunny and warm, but Veronica saw nothing but overcast skies and drizzling rain. She didn't realize that her negativity was sabotaging every part of her life. She was gorgeous, but couldn't keep a boyfriend; she was smart, but settled for a low-paying job; and even when good things happened, she found something to complain about. I'm still trying to help her see that an upbeat attitude would make her gloomy existence a whole lot brighter.

Granted, I'm not saying that my life is nonstop rainbows and unicorns. I occasionally get lonely because I haven't yet realized my dream of getting married and starting a family. But I can snap out of that funk pretty quickly just by looking at all the good things my past relationships have brought me. I was with one woman for eight years and we're still good friends today. Yes, we hung on a little too long but I wouldn't have traded that time with her for anything. I then fell in love with another amazing woman who made a difference in my life in so many ways. Even though my feelings for her may never be reciprocated the way I'd like them to be, I feel lucky to have felt that kind of love. Just because a relationship ends doesn't means it wasn't successful. I know with certainty that everything I've learned and experienced with every woman I've been with has prepared me for the day when I do meet the woman I'm going to spend forever with. And after doing the work I did with Brenda, my therapist, I know I'll find a woman who will value me now that I value myself.

That's a key point. Feeling worthy of success is the foundation for building a successful life. The idea to write this book popped into my head a few years ago, but I brushed it aside, thinking, *Who am I to write a book? Who's going to read it? I don't have anything to say.* Obviously, I wasn't ready to tackle it yet. But as I worked on myself and reflected on all the life and business lessons I had learned and how they could help others, I started thinking that writing a book wasn't such a dumb idea after all.

So I drew up a list of pros and cons. The pros column had one item: "Because I want to." The list of cons filled the whole column: "I'm not interesting enough." "I'm not a great speaker." "I don't have a college degree." "I'm not good-looking enough." Right away, I started challenging each con: "What do you mean you're not a good speaker? Why do you feel that way? What proof do you have? Remember, you won awards in high school contests." One by one, I scratched out every single objection. When the last one had been erased, I said to myself, *Looks like it's time to write that book.*

A lot of other great things have happened since that day. I created an entertainment website featuring celebrity interviews and profiles. I'm getting booked to give inspirational speeches. I'm producing a movie, which I never imagined myself doing. I started another lighting company with two partners (we lit up Usher and Maroon 5 for the Super Bowl). I'm traveling all over the world. And all of this became possible simply because I was willing to shake up my belief structure. It may not have been easy, but ultimately it comes down to a simple concept: Change the way you look at the world, and your world changes.

Living Without Limits
Your Life, Your Thoughts

- When others have poured cold water on your dreams, what was it deep inside of you that refused to give up?

- If warnings and discouragements from naysayers have held you back from pursuing your dreams, what can you do right now to break free from that negativity and follow your dreams?

- How can you shift your focus from trying to protect what ultimately can't be protected to experiencing all that life has to offer?

- Who are the people in your life who are the best role models for living authentic, adventurous lives?

- How can you be a source of encouragement and support for others who are in need of it?

- What value do you think you would receive and be able to offer by mentoring others?

- What are three things you can start doing today to develop a more positive approach to life?

- How can you start seeing and interpreting other people's feelings and intentions more clearly instead of distorting them through the lens of your own self-image?

- How can you make introspection a more regular part of your daily life?

- Looking objectively at your self-image as if it were someone else's, what elements of it no longer serve you and need to be overwritten with new messages?

- What are some positive qualities that other people see in you that you have a hard time seeing in yourself?

- How do you think your interactions with people would change if you started looking for reasons to admire everyone you meet?

- What's the most amazing thing you learned about somebody that you never would have expected given your initial impression of them?

- In what ways can you encourage people to see more beauty in their lives?

- Why will other people value you more when you value yourself more?

- Why is there no such thing as a failed relationship?

- In what ways can you imagine that your world will change when you change the way you look at the world?

RETURN TO SENDER

My mother was a homemaker who always stayed close to home. She didn't drive and didn't pursue any interests outside of her family. I realize now that she spent a lot of time waiting for my dad to come home from work, or for one of her three boys to get home and drive her somewhere. But I don't ever remember her complaining. She just kept on cleaning and organizing and making sure our home was perfect.

My mother is why I'm so conscientious about not keeping people waiting. I saw what it was like on the other end to be waiting for someone or something. Promptly responding to others is more than just common courtesy; it's a sign of respect and a tangible way to convey to others that they are worthy of your attention.

Not keeping people waiting is also one of the biggest reasons behind my professional success.

That's no exaggeration. For example, shortly after I began working full time at Advanced Lighting, I got a voicemail from Tony at Rose Brand, a distributor of stage products for Broadway shows. At that point, we had not done business with them but they were a major player in the industry. Establishing them as a customer would be huge. In his message, Tony asked if I wanted to bid on a project. The second after the message ended I was dialing Tony back. He said, "Wow! That was quick! I thought you were busy." I said, "I'm not too busy for business." He told me the project specs, I whipped up a bid, and an hour later I got the job. Later on, Tony told me that he had sent the same request for information to two of my competitors; I already had a purchase order before the other lighting companies had even responded.

By responding lightning-bolt fast, I had positioned Advanced Lighting in the mind of my new customer as the go-to provider of fiber optic curtains. Tony couldn't help but think, *They're quick, they're responsive, and they take care of business.* From that point on, Tony asked me to bid on every job that came up. Each time, I responded quickly with a proposal and quotes. Finally, after I'd delivered four quality projects, Tony called and suggested that we formally partner up. He told me that Rose Brand's CEO trusted Advanced Lighting enough to put some checks and balances in place, bypass the bidding process, and make us their exclusive fiber optic curtain supplier. As time went on, our partnership with Rose Brand deepened and evolved; they'd fly us in to train their employees and include us as part of their team at trade shows. We earned that trust and access by being responsive, doing what we said we were going to do, and delivering on time.

It's not an understatement to say that hooking up with Rose Brand changed my life. When Tony gave me that first order, Advanced Lighting was doing around $300,000 in sales and no one knew who we were. We quickly moved to well over a million dollars in sales and everyone knew our name because Rose Brand allowed us to put our name on our curtains. That branding opportunity gave us instant credibility and visibility, which enabled us to research and develop other lighting products for other markets, and that's when Advanced Lighting really got going. All of that might never have happened had I waited a day to return that phone call.

The way I see it, people aren't going to contact you just to waste their time. They're reaching out to you because they want you to answer a question that's important to them. You can't assume how important that question will be to you or what it may lead to, so treat every message or inquiry like it can make or break your business. Because it can.

Responding immediately to messages gives you a competitive edge that even your toughest competitors can't erase. I can't tell you how many times a customer has said to me, "Hey, I just sent that e-mail. Thanks for getting back to me so quickly." My response is always, "Of course. Your business is very important to me." If that customer were you, you'd be thinking, *Wow, anyone this responsive is going to give really good service. This is the kind of good, reliable company I'm looking for.*

Every voicemail, every e-mail, and every text opens a window of opportunity to make that kind of lasting impression on someone. You have to act as if that window is about to slam shut at any moment. Wait even just an hour, and you leave that window open for everybody else that person has contacted for information about products and services. Granted, getting back to people at the speed of light doesn't guarantee results; but it does put you in position to get the best results possible. Do that consistently, and success can't help but find you.

If your company has a good-size sales staff, put my theory to the test. Give ten salespeople a phone message five minutes before lunchtime or quitting time. It's a safe bet that the top two earners will return that call immediately, and that most of the other eight will call after lunch or the next morning. It's a matter of being other-centered versus self-centered. If you'd like to know what separates the remarkables from the replaceables, that's a good place to start.

People who are other-centered are self-aware; they understand the value of humility and service to others. They know that when they act in someone else's best interests, they're ultimately acting in their own best interests.

People who are self-centered are unaware; they seek first to serve themselves and their own ego. It doesn't occur to them that waiting to return a message not only hurts the customer asking the question, it may also hurt the customer of that customer and the customer of that customer. They have no idea of the damage they do when they passively allow themselves to become a bottleneck.

From time to time, I've done business with people who seem incapable of returning calls and e-mails. When I follow up, the person always laughs it off, saying, "Oh, I'm just not good at that." There's a word for people like that, and trust me, the word isn't "successful." I can understand if someone doesn't know the answer to a question or doesn't have the time to provide a detailed response, but that's still no excuse. It takes just seconds to e-mail back, "Got it, I'm on it. I'll get back to you soon."

Let's say a customer calls but you're rushing off because your kid is sick and needs to be picked up at school. Sending a quick e-mail can make all the difference: "Hi, got your call. Need to take care of a family matter but will call you back ASAP. Your business is important to me." You just acknowledged that you received the call, told him he's important, and that you're going to get back to him. You reinforced the relationship while also letting him know your family is a top priority. You get an A+ in customer care.

It's maddening trying to work with someone who is unresponsive. Not long ago, I was involved in a creative writing project that I was super excited about. But my enthusiasm soon gave way to frustration because the project lead was so horrible about returning messages. Every time my input was required, I'd do what was needed, then fire off an e-mail with action items to the project lead. More often than not, I may as well have sent my e-mail to a black hole in a galaxy far, far away. Four or five days would go by and I'd hear nothing. That's inexcusable on so many levels. It was not only frustrating as hell, it put me in the uncomfortable position of having to contact him again to ask if he got my first message. It was also unhealthy for the project because his unresponsiveness caused needless delays and changed my mindset from inspired to infuriated. His poor communication skills cost me time and money, and I didn't like it.

The next time you're tempted to dash out the door to lunch or the golf course before returning a call or an e-mail, remind yourself that your business is not about you, it's about making other people feel valued. When your customers, vendors, and employees feel valued, they in turn will value their interactions with you and what you have to offer. Making someone feel valued and cared for strengthens that relationship; and your success in business, just as your happiness in life, is determined by the quality of your relationships.

Ultimately, how you act in your professional life reveals a lot about what's important to you in your personal life. For instance, every time I respond promptly to a message, I'm not only honoring the person I'm replying to, I'm in some small way honoring my mother as well, and atoning for all the times I unintentionally kept her waiting.

Return To Sender
Your Life, Your Thoughts

- What is the message you're sending to someone when you respond promptly to their voicemail or e-mail?

- What is the message you're sending to someone when you don't respond promptly to their voicemail or e-mail?

- Why is responding immediately to all inquiries such a competitive differentiator?

- What other qualities would you associate with a business that got back to you at the speed of light?

- What does your attitude about responding to others tell you about yourself?

- Why is responding quickly to messages so integral to building quality relationships?

MISSION CONTROL

When Robin, the small-business owner I was advising, told me, "God, there aren't enough hours in the day!" I knew exactly what ailed her. Perpetually racing against the clock is a symptom of the dreaded disease that's taken down many a business leader: do-it-yourself-itis. Sure enough, Robin moaned that she was so buried in paperwork and taking care of every last detail at her PR firm that she often didn't get home until eleven at night. I listened patiently, then said, "Robin, work is not the problem; you are. Don't you have people you can delegate to?" Sheepishly, she said, "Yeah, I know I need to get better at that. I just want everything to be done right."

I pointed out that there were four big reasons why devoting so much of her time to getting the little things totally right was totally wrong: "First of all, there are people out there who can do those little things better than you can. Find them, hire them, and leave them alone. Second, every hour you're doing something other than your core competencies of landing clients and coming up with great ideas, you're costing yourself money. Third, if you're sweating in the trenches instead of climbing up the mountaintop, you won't notice all the opportunities that are there for the taking. Fourth, if you don't enjoy doing bookkeeping or HR functions but you're doing them anyway, you're not going to be happy. When you're out there meeting clients and going to special events, you come alive because that's what you love to do. People will pick up on that and gravitate toward you."

I also nudged Robin toward reframing her situation so she could shift from feeling stressed to feeling blessed. "It's not the work that's creating all these problems, it's how you're looking at and dealing with things," I said. "Do you know how fortunate you are to have all this work that's making you so tense? So many businesses are struggling and yours is booming. The only thing you're doing wrong is tackling so much of it by yourself. And given that you're planning on expanding into New York and L.A., you need to master this now or you'll be even more of a wreck. Ultimately, you can play the victim card but all you're doing is appeasing your conscious mind; your subconscious mind knows that you brought this on yourself. You won't get to where you want to go or be who you want to be until you consciously take ownership of your thoughts and actions."

I told Robin to think of her business as a movie and that it was up to her to cast all the roles. "Would

you cast yourself as a receptionist or a bookkeeper?"
I asked. "Well, if you're performing any of those
tasks, you're miscasting your movie; you don't see
Julia Roberts playing an extra in a crowd scene. As
the person in charge, the only thing that matters is
that you're doing the things that matter."

After we hung up, Robin texted me to say I had
fired her up and that she was determined to be a
champion delegator. I was glad to hear that because
I hate seeing people make the same mistakes that
kept me running in place for so long. I used to be a
control freak at my business too, not realizing that
keeping my hands in everything limited my own
growth as well as that of my company. It wasn't
until I released my insecurities and hired Marlon
as controller that I felt liberated to focus more of
my attention on sales and marketing—the things I
loved and did best. I used to spend hours going over
the books, running numbers, consulting with my
accountant, learning software, and wondering how
I was going to produce the information I needed and
whether I was even doing it right. Now all I had to
do was tell Marlon the info I wanted, and boom!
the report would be on my desk.

I had a tougher time a few years later when
I hired a sales manager. Sales was hard for me to
give up but the company had grown so much that
I needed to take a big-picture approach and devote
more time to client and vendor relationships. Even
so, I thought, *Wait a minute. Someone's going to come in
and tell me how to sell my product?* Well, guess what?
He did and he actually knew more about it than I

did because that was his area of expertise. In the past, I'd put my sales manager hat on for an hour or two here and there, but you can bet I was also thinking about the books . . . and inventory . . . and shipping . . . and everything else because those were the hats I was going to put on next. My new sales manager only worried about one thing: sales.

Giving up control of the universe had a nice side benefit: it forced me to be more responsible for my time. Just like Robin was feeling, I'd often think, *God, there aren't enough hours in the day!* But the more top-notch people I hired, the more I started finding myself with extra time on my hands. I remember sitting at my desk one day thinking, *What's going on? We're busy, we're growing, and there's nothing I've gotta do right now.* That's when I realized I had been fooling myself all those years. Back then, I subconsciously thought I deserved to be successful just because I was working so hard and putting in fourteen-hour days. I remember my parents telling me, "You're such a hard worker. We're so proud of you, Paul." But that didn't mean my business was profitable; it just meant I put in a lot of hours and I was exhausted. Don't get me wrong, working hard is an absolute requirement but it's not the number of hours you work that's important, it's what you accomplish in those hours.

Once that lesson clicked, I got into the habit of asking myself throughout the day, *Is what I'm doing right now moving me toward my long-term goals?* If I was moving left or right instead of straight ahead, I reminded myself that I couldn't be the visionary I needed to be if I was buried up to my neck in paper-work and doing everyone else's job. I can laugh about it now, but I had been so adamant about learning to perform every aspect of every job in the company. I remember the day that changed. A client asked me to hook up his new LED fixtures, but I hadn't gone to the effort to learn how to do that job as well as it needed to be done. I said, "You know what, I've got the perfect guy for that back at the office. Let me get him on the phone." And then I let the expert do his thing.

I also jumped at opportunities to train my team to be aware of how they spent their time. For instance, Marlon used to literally spend hours try-ing to save a dollar or even less. I finally told him, "Marlon, if this is a recurring product that we buy that we need lots of, sure, we'll worry about the dol-lar. But if it's something that we buy once a year, don't worry about it. How much do you make per hour? How about me? This fifteen-minute conver-sation about saving a dollar probably cost us thirty bucks, not to mention preventing us from doing something more valuable with our time. In a case like this, a penny saved is a dollar wasted."

If you're still throwing on and yanking off dif-ferent hats all day long and working past dark, you may be unwittingly spinning your wheels like Robin was. The deeper you sink into that rut, the harder you think you have to work. Over time, your best efforts may not only become ineffective but counter-productive. Yet, adding one more thing to your To Do list—even if it's *Do something about all these things on my To Do list*—only weighs you down further. Here's a three-word solution: divide and conquer. Trying to make too many changes at once will only make you more frazzled. On the other hand, if you think you're too crazy busy to make *any* changes and that you'll get around to it someday, I can assure you that "someday" will never come. Instead of an all-or-nothing approach, choose one small step you can take *today* to move you in the right direction. Work on that for a week, then pick another small mental or physical adjustment to test out. Do that every week and before you know it, your mountain of problems will have been reduced to a little pile of pebbles. Goodbye rut, hello freedom!

Mission Control
Your Life, Your Thoughts

- Why is it counterproductive to think that you are the only one who can get everything done the right way?

- How can delegating take you from feeling stressed to feeling blessed?

- If you are resisting delegating, why is that evidence that you're not living as consciously as you could be?

- If you think of your business as a movie, have you cast all the roles correctly, beginning with your own?

- How can giving up control help you get back in control?

- How can you remind yourself throughout the day to make the best use of your time?

- What is a minor responsibility that you can delegate right now?

TAKE THE HIGH ROAD

Four years after Kelly Jones had tried to overthrow me, I found myself downing a few beers with Frank, whose wife Cheryl had been one of my best employees at Advanced Lighting. After comparing notes about our Harleys, Frank got serious for a moment. "Paul, I want to tell you something," he said "Cheryl was happiest when she worked for you. And now that she's worked for other people, she realizes what an incredible boss you were." I told him how much I appreciated that and we started reminiscing about the Advanced Lighting days.

When Frank mentioned what a con artist Kelly was, I just shrugged and said that she must have had an awfully painful life and that I wished her the best. With a little smile, I added, "But I will tell you one thing. I've got a recording of your voice screaming how fired I am." It was true. When Kelly had left me angry voicemail messages during her last night in Sauk Centre, I could hear Frank in the background yelling, "You are so fired!" Frank grinned sheepishly and said, "Well, I'll be honest with you, Paul," he said. "Kelly had a lot of us convinced that you were a bad guy." I smiled and said, "Well, at least now you know what a great guy I am." And we high-fived and laughed about it.

Over the years, I had plenty of opportunities to exact revenge on Frank if I had wanted to. He had come to me looking for a donation to help build a local dog park, and instead of slamming the door in his face I pledged $500. I'm an animal lover and had just lost my dog so I was happy to pitch in. I had also given Frank and Cheryl $2,000 worth of kitchen flooring that was left over from the building of my house. I had never held Frank's alliance with Kelly against him. I had told myself, *You know what, he's young and impressionable. I'm not proud of everything I did when I was younger either.*

Actually, if anyone had a right to be resentful, it was Frank and Cheryl, not me. Two years after I sold Advanced Lighting, the new owners relocated, let everyone go, and closed the Sauk Centre facility. That's the last thing I wanted to see happen, but it was beyond my control; I had been let go myself by that time. I'd understand if a former employee blamed me for losing their job; but to Frank and Cheryl's credit, they recognized that I was acting in their best interests at the time and that not everything turns out the way you hope it will.

Frank and I can laugh and share a beer today because of a lesson my parents taught me years ago: Take the high road. It's not just the honorable thing to do, it's also the healthiest choice you can make. In fact, I can think of six reasons why it's better to carry my head held high instead of carrying a grudge.

First, doing the right thing helps maintain my integrity and self-respect. I know the kind of person I want to be—kind, compassionate, and loving—and I won't let anyone else's misguided actions prevent me from living up to my own expectations. I can't control other people's behavior but I sure can control mine.

Second, choosing empathy over enmity is good for my health. Scores of studies have shown how anger and resentment spike your blood pressure, compromise your immune system, and make you more susceptible to heart attacks and strokes. I love the way author Malachy McCourt put it: "Resentment is like taking poison and waiting for the other person to die."

Third, the cost of not forgiving someone is my own peace of mind. If I had resented Frank for siding with Kelly against me, I'd always be dreading the thought of running into him around town. I'm not a big fan of tense encounters. I'd much rather greet people with a friendly smile instead of a clenched fist.

Fourth, I see relationship challenges as tests to see how well I'm walking my talk. It's easy to be positive and caring when someone is being positive and caring toward me. But I will never fully be the loving, caring person I want to be until I can care about people who are acting in uncaring ways.

Fifth, I try to view every conflict as an important life lesson. When I heard Frank yelling on that phone call, I told myself it was a good reminder to look past the pettiness that can get the best of all of us and look for the goodness that's in every human heart.

Sixth, taking the high road just might inspire the person who mistreated me to take a look at her own behavior and start making better choices. If she's not ready to be awakened yet, at least I'm planting a seed. Hopefully, a few kind words from other people down the road will help that seed to sprout.

Ultimately, taking the high road always leads me to a good place. I feel happier and more peaceful, and I've learned that former enemies can become valued friends. I only wish I had discovered that secret sooner. After years of giving in to anger and resentment, I now know where the high road can be found—and that the bridges you burn are the very bridges leading to it.

Take The High Road
Your Life, Your Thoughts

- Why does holding a grudge give the person you're upset with even more control over your life?

- Why is forgiveness good for your health?

- Why does resentment prevent you from experiencing true happiness and peace?

- In what ways does someone doing you wrong offer valuable lessons in how to view and treat others?

- How does taking the high road potentially impact those who have mistreated you?

SECTION III

GETTING PERSONAL

*Your most personal life experiences have played
a big role in shaping who you are as a person—
and who you are determines how you show up
in the workplace.*

SUMMER OF SHAME

In the summer between fourth and fifth grade, my childhood innocence and sense of self were mangled beyond repair in the space of twenty minutes.

My family and I were visiting some family friends who lived twenty miles away. Whenever we saw them, and it was pretty often, I'd go play in the field behind their house with Mary, a girl my age who lived next door. On the other side of the field behind a bunch of shrubs and trees, there was an alleyway and then some stores and a gas station. The hardware store must have sold refrigerators because we'd often find huge cardboard boxes in the alley to play with.

One day, a few older kids who must have been around eighteen walked by and stopped. They talked amongst themselves for a few minutes and then approached us with smiles on their faces. Before Mary and I knew what was going on, they had forced us into the refrigerator box and told us to take off our clothes or else they would beat us up. They made us kiss each other and take turns touching each other before they ran off laughing, but not before they told us they would kill us and our families if we told anyone. Mary and I threw on our clothes and ran back home. We were too embarrassed to talk about what just happened but I'm sure Mary felt the same way I did: weird, ashamed, and completely disoriented.

My family visited our friends almost every weekend that summer, and the same scenario happened two or three more times. Each time, they threatened us and made us do even more graphic stuff to each other. They even told us to simulate sex, which we had no idea how to do.

Whenever I saw the boys walking toward us, I felt paralyzed with fear and dread. Looking back, I understand now that I felt completely helpless and that the only way for me to endure the torture was to go numb so I wouldn't feel anything. I think on some level I pretended it hadn't happened because I was just too young to process it in any rational way. It felt like some door inside of me had slammed shut and even I wasn't allowed to go inside. If anyone watched me that summer, I'm sure they thought I was just a normal kid living a normal life; I still played with my neighborhood friends and laughed and ran around just like everybody else.

I didn't realize it at the time, of course, but you can only suppress a traumatic experience for so long. It's like trying to hold a beach ball under water; without warning, it'll shoot to the surface and there's nothing you can do to stop it. Looking back, that explains why I felt so alienated when school started again. Walking down the halls, I felt like everyone was staring at me, *like they knew*. I felt like I was in a slow-motion movie and everybody was pointing at me and laughing. But there was no place to run and no place to hide.

The second day of school, Tim and David, two kids from my neighborhood, ganged up on me and said they were going to kick me out of Cub Scouts. They were just trying to intimidate me but I was sure it was because they knew what had happened with Mary and me. I didn't ask them if they knew because if I did and they didn't, then they *would* know. I just said, "That's fine, I don't want to be in it anyways." And I stopped going on my own, just like I stopped going to football practice the month before.

That first week of school, my panic and paranoia kicked into high gear. I did everything I could—I cried, I pretended I was sick, I refused to get on the bus—to avoid going to school. My parents would take me to school and I would go running out the other door. My parents obviously worked something out with the school because I eventually wound up in a classroom all by myself with my own private teacher. Maybe they all thought I was just going through a phase and needed some special attention. Then again, based on my grade school history, it was clear that I had difficulty learning in traditional ways. Fortunately for me, Mrs. Lindgren was a great lady and I felt comfortable with her right away.

Having my own private teacher calmed me down big time. For the next six months, I felt almost normal. I had classes and homework just like everybody else and we even went on field trips to the zoo and a museum. Once we even went to a movie, just the two of us. I remember feeling very lucky that day. I liked Mrs. Lindgren a lot and grew very attached to her. In some ways, I think I learned a lot more than I would've learned in regular classes.

Even though I didn't fight going to school anymore, I was still nervous and introverted around my classmates. Whenever I had to mingle with them in the hallways, I felt super anxious. At home, I had returned to normal in the sense that I was very social with friends and relatives, but at school I would just shut down.

It was around that time I convinced myself that I wasn't very smart. Every bad grade I had ever gotten had clobbered my self-image and made my expectation of getting poor grades a self-fulfilling prophecy. On top of all that, I was in a special class, which to me meant special education, which meant I was a dumb kid and a reject. Having my own private teacher actually had nothing to do with my intelligence, but it took me years to realize that and even longer to accept it, especially since I was later placed in special education classes from junior high all the way through high school. It's funny how once we get an idea in our heads as kids how difficult it is to shake it even after we find out that it wasn't true. I've since come to understand that I'm just as smart as most people; I just learn in different ways.

I remember the day things started getting better. Mrs. Lindgren and I were eating lunch in the cafeteria just like we did every day after all the other students had left. Brian, a kid I barely knew, had left his lunchbox behind so he came back to retrieve it. When he saw me, his face brightened and he said, "Hey, Paul! We sure miss you in class. I hope you come back soon." I remember Mrs. Lindgren watching my reaction; I think she could tell that something had shifted in me. She said to me, "Well, how do you feel about that?" I said, "I don't know, maybe they want me back." She must have called my parents because I remember having a discussion with them when I got home. They asked me if I wanted to try going back to regular class and I said, "Sure." I did, and I never looked back.

Every so often, Mrs. Lindgren would come and find me to check on how I was doing. I remember talking to her at lunch a few times. I had thought she was a regular teacher but I guess she worked exclusively with children who had psychological issues. One day she told me that she wouldn't be coming back anymore. I got scared and said, "Where are you going? You can't go, I need you." She told me that she had gotten a good job elsewhere and that she was proud of how well I was doing and that I didn't need her anymore.

I didn't see Mrs. Lindgren again until I was in junior high two or three years later. I don't recall most of the details; all I remember is that we had a nice conversation for an hour or so and that she told me some things that have stuck with me ever since.

When I described how my life was going and the kinds of things that made me happy, she said I was an incurable romantic. That made me feel good, even though I admitted that I didn't know what it meant. She explained that I looked at everything in life in a romantic way and that I romanced life itself. That made me feel really special, like I had discovered something that the other kids hadn't. She said that it was okay that I didn't get all A's and B's because I was getting an A+ in life. She also told me that I had an ability to touch people and that I was sent here to inspire and help others. When I left, I felt like I was floating on air. Mrs. Lindgren was the first person to recognize those qualities in me and I am so grateful to her for making such a huge difference in my life.

In hindsight, this terrible thing that happened to me that made me so self-conscious and weak ultimately made me stronger and wiser. I learned a whole lot about myself that I might not have ever come to understand if I hadn't been damaged so profoundly. I'm certainly not saying that I'm glad it happened; I wish it hadn't, both for my sake and for Mary's. But I've learned that I need to take whatever life throws at me, good or bad, learn what I can from it, and keep moving.

I know that the abuse I suffered doesn't compare to so many of the sexual abuse horror stories out there, but it was abuse just the same. Like those other cases, it wasn't about sex so much as it was about somebody taking away all your power and putting you under their complete control. It's an awful feeling and my heart goes out to anyone who's experienced anything like it. I was so traumatized by it that I never talked about what happened until five years ago with my therapist. It's still difficult for me to talk about; I never did tell my parents. I wish I could have before my mom passed away because they probably blamed themselves for all the trouble I had back in fifth grade.

The effects of those experiences lingered for many years and probably still do to some extent. When I started dating and having girlfriends, I felt dirty somehow, like my virginity was gone and I couldn't get it back or be wholesome ever again. Those negative thoughts and fears infiltrated my belief system and explain why I unwittingly sabotaged so many relationships later on in life. My subconscious was telling me, "I can't have that, I don't deserve that, I'm not smart enough, I was a dirty little boy and I'm not worthy of that." It took a lot of time and therapy to work through all that and get to the point where I realized that I am a good person and that I am worthy of having a loving relationship and a wonderful family. In fact, as soon as I started dealing with these issues, a lot of great things started happening, from cashing out of my business to finding more peace and happiness in my life to more consciously being of service to others. I feel like my life has come full circle, and I know a lot of that is due to coming to terms with what happened to me when I was a little boy.

Summer Of Shame
Your Life, Your Thoughts

- If you experienced a childhood trauma, how did it change your outlook and the way you interacted with people?

- How did your most difficult childhood experiences affect your self-esteem?

- In what ways did you feel different than all the other kids at school?

- What ideas did you have about yourself as a child that you later realized were untrue?

- When and where did you feel most accepted during your childhood?

- Outside of your immediate family, who were the adults who most influenced you as a child?

- What difficult events in your childhood ultimately taught you important life lessons?

- Nowadays, when you feel powerless or vulnerable, in what ways can you trace those feelings back to your childhood?

- In what ways have you sabotaged various areas of your life?

- What do you feel your friends and loved ones deserve that you don't?

- In what ways is the child you used to be holding your current self hostage?

- What events or feelings from your childhood do you still need to come to terms with?

WRESTLING WITH FEAR

At nine years old, I learned something important about myself: I was a quitter. I had been quarterback of my Pee Wee Football team the past two years and a new season was about to get underway. When I found out that my family wouldn't get back from an August family vacation until three days after practice had started, I begged my dad to change our plans, but he held firm. I was really nervous about playing football again with for reasons I didn't understand (and wouldn't understand until years later when I came to terms with the abuse I had suffered earlier that summer). A few words of encouragement from my dad would have at least helped me keep my insecurity in check; his apparent indifference made me even more upset.

The morning after we returned from vacation, my dad drove me to practice. Despite my plea to get there on time, we were running late. As we approached the park and I saw my uniformed team-mates doing jumping jacks, my fears about losing my starting quarterback position and not fitting in shifted into overdrive. I couldn't stand the thought of showing up late for practice on top of missing the first three days altogether. What would the kids think? What would they say? Boom, I launched into full panic mode right there in the front seat of my dad's Buick.

Sobbing, I begged my dad to turn around but he ignored me. I was out of control, yelling at him to take me back home. I remember looking at the kids and feeling like I was watching a movie in slow motion; every jumping jack seemed to take ten seconds. I was getting more frantic by the second: I screamed at my dad that I wouldn't get out of the car. He was furious. The look on his face told me he was ashamed of me, which only intensified my panic. Finally, he gave in and turned the car around. Those few minutes of slouching in the front seat on the way home and seeing my dad's look of disappointment pretty much destroyed me.

I felt awful about myself for abandoning football. My confidence bottomed out and I soon found myself bailing out in other challenging situations. The funny thing about quitting was, the more I did it the easier it got. In fact, it started to seem almost natural, like it was part of my DNA.

Ironically, after wrestling with insecurity, it was wrestling that helped me feel secure again. My brother Jerry, who's four years older than me, was a talented wrestler and I wanted to follow in his footsteps and impress him. So I had joined AAU (Amateur Athletic Union) Wrestling the summer before fourth grade. It was a summer program that was unaffiliated with the school district; none of my classmates were there so I wasn't worried about embarrassing myself in front of people I knew. As my wrestling skills improved throughout my grade school years, I started gaining confidence again. Jerry was always at the end of the mat during my matches; when my head was down I'd see his eager eyes urging me on. He'd pound the mat and shout, "Go! Go!" That fired me up so much I hardly ever lost.

I was a good wrestler because I was skinny and wiry and quick. Thanks to my AAU experience, when I hit junior high I was recruited for the varsity wrestling team. As a seventh grader, I was wrestling seniors and getting my share of pins, although my overall winning percentage was only around .500. In eighth grade, I only lost twice and just missed going to state. My most indelible memory from that season was wrestling a senior from North High, which was located in a rough area of Minneapolis. In regular high school wrestling, you try to take your opponent down and pin him. In AAU freestyle wrestling, you try to score points by controlling your opponent—you take him down, let him back up, and take him down again. Just for fun, I wrestled this kid as if we were in AAU. I kept on taking him down, letting him back up again, and basically just screwing with him because I could. Finally, he got so frustrated that he jumped up and punched me in the nose. I was bleeding everywhere and he got disqualified. At first I thought it was pretty funny but then, to my horror, I realized that, just like the older boys who toyed with Mary and me three years earlier, I was guilty of controlling somebody else for my own amusement. I still feel badly about that. I'm lucky that the only price I had to pay was a bloody nose.

In ninth grade, I lost just once and qualified for state; the guy who eventually beat me ended up taking first in state in my weight class. I was getting scouted by some top wrestling colleges and feeling pretty good about myself. In fact, a teammate and I had gained fame as the Cradle Brothers because we won all our matches by pinning opponents with the cradle technique. We were mini-celebrities at all the meets.

Then it all fell apart. I got sick in tenth grade with some sort of intestinal disease. It took forever for doctors to figure out how to fix it and I missed the entire wrestling season. When wrestling started up again in eleventh grade, it was déjà vu time. Just like the summer before fifth grade with football, I felt super self-conscious after missing so much time. Plus, I'd lost my celebrity status. My insecurities and fear of failure bubbled to the surface and started raging out of control: *Everyone else has got another year on me now. What if I come back and I'm not as good? I'd be so embarrassed because I used to be on top.*

I chickened out and reverted back to my pattern of quitting when things got tough. I still had a lot of interest from wrestling colleges but that was actually a big reason why I quit. I was afraid that if I got a scholarship, I'd have to go to college and everybody would find out I wasn't very smart.

It seemed easy to quit wrestling because I had paved the way by quitting football. Except it turned out not to be so easy after all. My tendency for self-loathing intensified as time went on, especially when I saw the success that was coming to guys whom I had easily beat when I was in my prime. But it was too late to go back and I knew I'd always be kicking myself for being such a screw-up and a failure.

I finally developed some self-confidence after joining the Army Reserve and spending eight weeks at Basic Training the summer after my junior year (see the "Basic Training" chapter for the full story), but it was finding a mentor my senior year that really got me started down the road to redemption. One day in math class, I was screwing around at the blackboard with some other students and I accidentally broke a long piece of chalk into three pieces. The teacher got mad and said, "You just wasted that chalk." I said, "No I didn't. What I did was create two more pieces of chalk because we're running short and other people needed some chalk."

The teacher was impressed that I was so quick-witted, and so was Paul Bruchard, the retired businessman sitting in back who was observing the class. Paul had become active at the school in order to mentor and help students who showed promise. He recognized that, even though I wasn't the best of students, that I was a good kid. After class, he walked down the hall with me and said, "You're kind of bored with school, aren't you?" When I agreed, he said, "Why don't you come to my class? I think you'll really like it and learn a lot. And get this, if you get a job, you can get out of school early." That sounded awesome so I showed up in his class the next day.

Paul's class was actually the DECA program, which helps students prepare to be business leaders and entrepreneurs. Meeting Paul and joining DECA was life changing. I worked together with other students in career-building projects that taught us about sales, service, management, and other business functions. Paul also gave me tapes of Zig Ziglar, Earl Nightingale, and other motivational speakers, and I couldn't get enough of them. For the first time in my life, I was learning and loving it.

I was naturally glib and quick on my feet so one subject that came easily to me was simulating job interviews. I got so good at it that I found myself becoming a class leader, another first for me. One day it hit me: I'm excelling at something in school! I couldn't believe it. My parents noticed me changing too and were very supportive. Up till then, I hadn't given them much reason to be proud of me so that felt really, really good.

With Paul's encouragement, I entered the annual DECA competition in the Job Interview category and took first place at districts. I followed that up by winning state and regionals too. Every win gave me a huge self-esteem boost. I ended up taking third place at nationals and came back to school with a new level of confidence. Man, that felt good. That's when I started thinking, *Wow, I can do anything I want.*

I don't have to be an A student, I just have to be passionate about what I'm doing and believe in myself. I felt like Mark Twain had me in mind when he wrote, "Never let your schooling interfere with your education."

Thanks to Paul's guidance, I was able to smooth over the quitting pattern embedded in my brain and overwrite it with a new pattern that expected nothing less than winning. The lesson stuck. Today, it doesn't even occur to me that failing is a possibility.

Best of all, I no longer am fearful of fear. Knowing how scared and insecure I had been for so long now gives me the motivation and courage I need to keep moving forward, even if a big business deal or first date is in danger of imploding. Every time I feel fear bubbling up in me, I draw strength from it, knowing full well that any momentary discomfort is nothing compared to the shame and regret I'd feel for letting fear become my master. Today, I am proud to call fear my friend.

Wrestling With Fear
Your Life, Your Thoughts

- What incident from your childhood comes to mind when you think of feeling embarrassed in front of your peers?

- What did you do that made the situation worse and what could you have done to make it better?

- In what ways do you still feel the repercussions of that incident today?

- What were your greatest fears in your formative years?

- How did those fears get in the way of your happiness?

- How have those fears survived as patterns that are still compromising the quality of your life today?

- What fears are you still holding onto today even though you know they're not supported by reality?

- What are three things you can do right now to conquer those fears once and for all?

- What experiences and achievements in your life helped build your self-confidence?

- Who was the first adult who saw something special in you and took it upon themselves to encourage, teach, or guide you?

- What were your early experiences in finding a career path or area of interest that you were enthusiastic about and good at?

- When did you start believing in yourself and why?

BASIC TRAINING

I was a dreamer in high school. I fantasized about living in exotic places, meeting cool people, doing exciting things, and having all the trappings of a successful life. But I knew my dreams were just dreams; after all, I was insecure, I wasn't very smart, and I was a quitter. Despite my dreams, I was resigned to ending up as a small town auto mechanic, just like my dad. It was honest work and a steady paycheck, it just didn't satisfy my desire to build something all my own.

My dad had served in the military and so had a bunch of my uncles and my middle brother, Jerry. So joining the Army Reserve my junior year in high school and carrying on the family tradition seemed like the thing to do. I had always done what was expected of me, mostly because I didn't have any expectations for myself.

I remember telling myself that joining the military was a good way to honor my family. But looking back, I see now that I was trying to associate myself with something that I hoped would make my family proud. Plus, I was craving a sense of belonging and searching for something that would add significance and meaning to my life. I was tired of feeling like a loser and never achieving anything.

The split training option in the Army Reserve was perfect for me because it allowed me to go to Basic Training the summer after my junior year and then to AIT (Advanced Individual Training) the summer after I graduated. Right after my junior year ended in early June, I was told to report to the Minneapolis bus station, where I'd take a bus to the airport with the other recruits.

I didn't sleep too well the night before I was scheduled to leave; I was scared and worried about leaving home for boot camp. I was seventeen but I looked like I was fifteen and felt like I was twelve. It was a long night.

The next morning, my father dropped me off at the bus station. As I was unloading my bags, I glanced at his face and, for a second or two, I was overjoyed. He looked so proud of me! I hadn't given him much reason to feel much pride in a long, long time, and the look on his face made me feel like I was doing the right thing after all. Just that one little smile from him really took the edge off my fear.

When our plane touched down in South Carolina, we filed into military buses for the ride to Fort Jackson. As soon as I stepped off the bus, a big, muscular recruit in his mid-twenties ran up, gave me a hard shove against the side of the bus, and started cussing me out. I was really confused and scared because I didn't know what the hell was going on. I was wearing a Minnesota Vikings T-shirt and it turns out he was unhappy about the Vikes thrashing his Detroit Lions during the season. Since he was already demonstrating that he could beat me into the ground, I kept my mouth shut and hoped he'd get tired of using me as a punching bag. Luckily, a little guy in his thirties—who we later nicknamed Bullet because he always wore a bullet around his neck—stepped in between us and said with a Southern drawl, "Hey now, leave him alone; he's just a young kid."

It didn't take long for all the recruits to get into a routine. I was pretty athletic so the training was easier than I thought it would be. I turned out to be good with a rifle too, which also boosted my confidence. I had been so hung up on my academic failures that I hadn't given myself much credit for what I was good at.

Our drill sergeant, Sergeant Bigsby, was a bad-ass older guy: lean, hard-nosed, and rough. We were all scared of him and did exactly as we were told. We got very good at saluting and shouting, "Yes, drill sergeant!" (Six years later, when the movie *Full Metal Jacket* came out, I was mesmerized by R. Lee Ermey's performance as the drill sergeant. He looked and sounded *exactly* like Sergeant Bigsby. It was uncanny.)

South Carolina summers are very hot and humid so we'd get regular breaks and go hang out on a nearby gravel area. They called it a smoke break because a bunch of the guys smoked. Those of us who didn't just hung around doing nothing. One day, during a break, I don't know how I found the nerve but I walked up to our drill sergeant and said, "Sergeant Bigsby, we call this a smoke break but only half of us smoke. The rest of us should at least be able to eat some Life Savers." The other recruits froze. They all looked at me like I had lost my mind; I'm sure they expected him to kick my ass. Sergeant Bigsby just stood there looking at me, intense as ever. Finally, he said, "All right, everybody who isn't smoking can go to the PX and get Life Savers." Whoa. That felt awesome. It was a real turning point for me because it gave me a surge of self-confidence and got me thinking that I had more to offer than I thought I did. What was really cool is, from that point on, the other guys treated me like I was a leader.

That's saying a lot because a lot of the recruits weren't exactly angels. Back in 1981, a lot of guys joined the military on waivers, meaning they had been given a choice between the military and jail. So here I was, an innocent Midwestern boy, tossed in with a motley crew of shady and even danger-ous characters. Remember Mr. Bad-ass who threw me against the bus for wearing a Vikings shirt? He was a waiver guy. Big surprise. And there was some-thing about Bullet that just didn't feel right. He was a super-nice guy who seemed to know everything about the military but he was always getting into some sort of trouble. Believe me, there was no lack of drama on base.

I started getting into the groove of Basic Training and actually enjoyed it. I didn't even mind the CQ (Charge of Quarters) duty, which was overnight desk duty. One night when it was my turn to stay up all night, I heard a noise in the barracks, like someone was crying out, so I grabbed my flashlight and went to investigate. I made my way through the dark hallways and stairs, peeked around a corner, and couldn't believe what I saw: There was Sergeant Bigsby beating Bullet to a bloody pulp. He was just wailing on the poor guy. Naturally, my first instinct was to help Bullet; but I was alone, with no one to help me if things got out of hand. So I stayed out of sight.

The next morning, Sergeant Bigsby told us that Bullet was no longer in our platoon and was being sent home for being a liar and a cheater. I felt a bit conflicted because of what I knew but I didn't feel comfortable about speaking up and didn't know if it would make any difference if I did. But it wasn't long before some guys from the Judge Advocate General's (JAG) Corps, the military's legal arm, came to our platoon and started asking questions. Obviously, they had interviewed Bullet about what had happened and intended to get to the bottom of it.

The JAG guys sat down with our group to see if anyone knew anything. They had pulled records and found out I had CQ duty the night Bullet got hurt, so they pulled me out of the room for a private interview. I may have been imagining it, but as I left the room I could have sworn that Sergeant Bigsby was staring me down with a look that said, "If you saw something, you didn't see anything."

I told the interrogator everything I saw, and even though they assured me that Sergeant Bigsby wouldn't be able to retaliate against me in any way, I was scared stiff for the next couple of weeks. Then one day we had a brand-new drill sergeant. He told us that Sergeant Bigsby had moved on to other things and that he was no longer a drill sergeant. But that wasn't the end of it. Right before Basic Training ended, the Jag Corps returned and I had to give an official deposition. It turns out that Sergeant Bigsby had a history of violent behavior; I heard his next tour of duty was military prison at Fort Leavenworth.

I felt a bit guilty about Sergeant Bigsby doing hard time because of the love/hate relationship recruits typically have with their drill sergeant. He pounded on us physically and emotionally day in and day out, but we knew he was doing it for our own good to make us better soldiers. Still, I knew right from wrong, and he definitely went over the line with Bullet. So even though I felt good about speaking up, I was still hoping and praying that no one would find out that I was the whistleblower. Thankfully, no one did because the military did a very good job of protecting me.

Basic Training
Your Life, Your Thoughts

- In your teenage years, how did you let other people's expectations define you?

- In what ways are you allowing other people's expectations to define you today?

- Which do you value more and why—taking pride in your actions or acting to make others proud?

- Why is it dangerous to value approval from others more than your own self-approval?

- What is the link between how you felt about leaving home for the first time and how you feel today about venturing into unknown territory?

- In what ways do you undervalue your strengths and overemphasize your weaknesses?

- What are your earliest memories of feeling self-confident and having others look up to you?

- In what ways do you initiate unnecessary drama in your life and the lives of others?

- What were the circumstances when you first found the courage to speak up and do what was right in a difficult situation?

SOLDIER OF THE YEAR

With eight weeks of Basic Training behind me, I showed up for my senior year of high school leaner, tougher, and more confident. I still struggled academically but my success in the military helped me realize that I had skills in other areas that could be just as valuable as book smarts.

As I got closer to graduation, it hit me that I was committed to learning diesel mechanics for my AIT (Advanced Individual Training) in the military that summer. But I wasn't interested in being a mechanic anymore. Thanks to DECA, I had options. I had gotten my first glimpse into the business world and I liked what I saw. Better yet, I thought I could be pretty good at it. But for two months that summer, I knew I had to be a good soldier and slog my way through AIT.

Right after graduation, I was flown to Aberdeen Proving Ground, the army facility near Aberdeen,

Maryland. We were stationed about twenty miles away at Post Edgewood, which was an old chemical plant. AIT wasn't as strict and as disciplined as Basic Training and the mechanic training came pretty easily to me.

Everything was fine except my feet were giving me problems. I had developed plantar warts and they got so bad that I was excused from physical activities. It turns out that getting plantar warts was one of the best things that ever happened to me because my drill sergeant told me, "You're not just going to sit on your ass, you're going to do some academics." For the next three weeks, he sat with me and tutored me in all sorts of subjects, from military history to current events. I actually enjoyed it and got along really well with my drill sergeant.

My feet were getting better so I figured I'd be returning to my regular platoon activities, but one day my drill sergeant surprised me by suggesting that I represent our platoon in the annual "Soldier of the Year" competition. He explained that every year, one AIT soldier from every branch of the military is selected to represent that branch in a competition. When he mentioned that a big part of the contest is based on academics, I told him he'd be better off finding someone a little smarter than me. I could fix an engine but that's about all I thought I could do. He didn't buy it. He said, "Guess what? You're going to do it because you're the only guy I have who can do it. The rest of them are idiots." I took that to mean I was the least idiotic of the bunch. With a compliment like that, how could I say no? Besides, it sounded like a direct order.

Next thing I knew, I was sitting down for interview sessions with base officers. I was asked a series of questions about the military, my job training, and current events. First I was matched against recruits in my own squad, then in my own platoon, and then in other platoons at Post Edgewood. The further along I got, the more confident I got; it felt like I was back in DECA, training for the Job Interview competition. I remember thinking, *Hey, I can do this. I'm good at this!* After coming out on top at Post Edgewood, I went head to head with the AIT recruit representing Aberdeen Proving Ground. Next thing I know, I'm being told, "Congratulations, you're representing the United States Army in the Soldier of the Year competition."

The next week passed in a blur. I spent every minute I could cramming for the final competition. It had all happened so fast that it didn't quite seem real. Me, representing the U.S. Army in *anything*? It was a good feeling but it took some getting used to.

Finally, the big day arrived. I was driven to another base where I found myself in a room with the representatives of the Air Force, Navy, Marines, and Coast Guard. I had been nervous that morning but now I felt a surge of confidence, like I was back in DECA, winning trophies.

I looked around the room, sizing up my competition. The Air Force guy was out of shape, his shoes looked average, and his gig line—the alignment of the shirt, belt buckle, and trouser fly—was bad.

The Coast Guard guy was chubby and his clothes were all wrinkly. The Navy guy looked good and the Marine guy looked awesome, like he was the walking definition of the word "military." I figured a few of them could beat me academically but I knew I looked almost as good as the Marine. The military is all about discipline and one of the most important standards is the way you look. Your uniform has to be perfect, from the way you lace your boots to the way your belt lines up with your zipper lining and the button line on your shirt. Mr. Marine and I were lapping the field in that department.

One by one, we were directed to a room where we would meet individually with a general who was the President of the Board. I watched with great interest as each of the first few candidates knocked on his door a few times. One of the things I had learned during my cram sessions was that when you report to the President of the Board in the military, you do so with a single knock on the door. So when my turn came, I gave one loud knock and waited . . . and waited. It was only for ten seconds or so but it seemed like ten minutes. Finally, he called out to me to enter. After I saluted and sat down, he said, "So what's with the knock? Didn't you hear the other men? They got my attention. You just knocked once." I told him that a single knock was the way to request a meeting with the President of the Board. He smiled and said, "Good job."

He then asked me general questions about my MOS (Military Occupation Specialties), which was wheel-vehicle repairman. After a few weeks of practice, I had my answers for that down pat. He followed up that line of inquiry with questions about the president of the U.S. that any grade school kid could have answered.

Then he hit me with, "What happened over the United States airwaves just recently?" I couldn't believe it. On the way over that morning, my drill sergeant and I were listening to news on the radio so I knew just how to respond. Without hesitation, I said, "Fidel Castro started broadcasting over our airwaves." He just looked at me, smiled, and said, "Very good. That will be all."

After the final candidate's interview, all of us were escorted to a holding room where we awaited the results along with our platoon leaders. I figured I did okay but expected to hear that I finished in the middle of the pack. The waiting was so nerve-wracking that any attempt we made at conversation seemed stiff and awkward. Finally, an officer stepped into the room and announced that this year was without precedent in the history of the award. He paused for a moment, then said, "The Army won it. Congratulations."

I was so surprised I just sat there with a goofy grin on my face. My drill sergeant was dumbfounded. He said, "I didn't think you had a chance in hell. We've never won. We've always been the black sheep." I don't remember much else after that until we were driving back to base. I think I was in shock.

On our way back, I noticed that my drill sergeant wasn't heading back to base. He smiled and said, "I've got a surprise for you." We pulled up near a helicopter, got in, and took off. A few minutes later, we landed in the middle of our base, where every single soldier was there waiting for us. They all saluted me as I stepped off the chopper.

That was a real highlight. I was also given a few hundred dollars in U.S. Savings Bonds and got a special weekend pass to ride in a helicopter along the shoreline near Chesapeake Bay. We flew right over the beaches while I leaned out to wave to people. It was phenomenal. I felt like a king.

I couldn't believe how far I had come from just the summer before when I was a scared little seventeen-year-old kid showing up for Basic Training. Every step along the way, from meeting Paul Bruchard to competing in DECA to army training to winning Soldier of the Year, kept moving me in the right direction, with each step laying the groundwork for the next one and building my confidence a little bit more. By the time I returned home from AIT, I knew there was a path somewhere that was a better fit for me than being a diesel mechanic. I had opened up my eyes and the world had opened up to me.

Soldier Of The Year
Your Life, Your Thoughts

- What were some apparent physical, emotional, or work-related setbacks that turned out to be blessings in disguise?

- What was the first time you threw yourself into a major challenge and were proud of your effort?

- What achievements are you most proud of and why?

- What are some defining moments from your teenage years that readied you for adulthood?

CONQUERING CANCER

I had been flying for American Airlines for three years and was at the top of my game. I was loving life and having fun. But life is fragile; it doesn't take much to go from feeling unstoppable and indestructible to feeling scared and vulnerable. All it took for me was feeling a little lump on my right testicle in the shower one morning.

When I mentioned the lump to my girlfriend, Janice, she insisted that I see a doctor. I was flying to Minnesota soon to visit my parents so I made an appointment at our family clinic in Minneapolis. I ended up seeing an older urologist who told me I had a little infection that would clear up with antibiotics. Five months later, the lump was still there so I made another trip to the clinic. The same doctor told me the same thing: I was fine and there was nothing to worry about.

Soon after that, I was talking to Joey, a fellow flight attendant who had recently gone through testicular cancer. When I asked him how he found out he had cancer, he said, "I found a little lump, went to the doctor, got an ultrasound and it showed up there." I called my clinic right away and booked another appointment, but this time I asked to see a different urologist. When I got in to see Dr. Kern, I told him I wanted an ultrasound. Since it was the third time I had been in, he approved the test.

At the medical center across the street, a young male radiology tech put some gel on me and started the ultrasound. Six or seven minutes into the procedure, he said, "I'll be right back." A few minutes later, in came a radiology tech who looked a little older. He examined me and said, "I'll be right back." A few minutes later, in came an M.D. in his forties with his radiology credentials on his lab coat. He looked things over and said the same four words: "I'll be right back." A few minutes later, in came an M.D. in his sixties with even more credentials on his lab coat. After examining me, he said, "Okay, we're done now." On one hand, I was impressed with all the attention but on the other hand, I was feeling pretty scared and apprehensive.

As I was getting ready to leave, the M.D. told me I needed to take the films over to my doctor. I said that Dr. Kern had told me that they would just send him a report. The tech was insistent. He said, "It's just across the street. It would be best if you took them over."

So I carried the films across the street and into the clinic. The office lobby was full of patients, but as soon as the nurse saw me, she jumped up and pulled me into Dr. Kern's private office. By this time I was feeling like a condemned man and wondering how many good months I had left. When Dr. Kern came in, he danced around the news for a couple of minutes before finally saying, "You've got a tumor the size of a centimeter in your right testicle. It doesn't mean it's cancer, but 95 percent of them are. If that's the case, we can insert a fake silicone testicle so you'll look and feel normal. I've got you scheduled for surgery at seven o'clock tomorrow morning." After absorbing that news for a minute, I stammered that I couldn't come back the next day because I was scheduled to fly a shift in the morning. He looked me in the eye and said two words: "Cancel it."

Dr. Kern also told me that in addition to the tumor in my right testicle, my left testicle had severe varicoceles, which are abnormally dilated testicular veins. That condition wasn't dangerous but it could make me sterile. He suggested that as long as we were going to do surgery on the right testicle, we might as well fix the left one as well. I managed to mumble, "Okay, go ahead."

I wandered out of his office in total shock. I felt like the ground had shifted beneath me and it was all I could do to keep my balance. I was looking at things and hearing people talk but nothing registered. It felt like I was sleepwalking. I heard the nurse's voice and realized that she was talking to me. "Paul, you're a young guy," she said. "Do you want to have children some day?" I nodded feebly, so she handed me a pamphlet about a local place called Cryogenic Laboratories. She could tell I was confused, so she explained that it was a sperm bank and that I should look into it because surgery could impair my fertility.

Still in a daze, I walked back across the street to the lobby of the medical office building and called my dad's car phone. I was still spaced out. I felt like I was in a movie, with the camera zooming in on me and everything else around me was just a blur. When my dad answered, I started crying pretty hard. I felt like the world was going to end and there was no hope for me. I told him I had a tumor, that I was having surgery in the morning, and asked if he could pick me up and take me to the cryogenic place. My parents lived across the border in Wisconsin but it didn't take him long to get there. We didn't say much to each other when I got into the car. We were both so shaken by the news that we were too disoriented to talk.

When we got to the cryogenic lab building, my dad waited in the car while I went inside. I rode the elevator up to the sixth floor and started walking down a long hallway. As I passed a handful of other businesses, I glanced at the receptionists through the little windows in their doors. I felt all their eyes on me and could hear their voices in my head: "We know where you're going. We know you're going to be masturbating into a jar." It was all so surreal, like a dream I couldn't wake up from. I felt like I was outside my body, watching myself go through the motions of walking down a hallway. I filled out the paperwork, did what I had to do, and returned to the car.

As we drove out of Minneapolis on the way to my parents' house in Wisconsin, the initial shock started wearing off. All the emotions that had been welling up inside of me were more than I could handle. I was feeling so overwhelmed, I just started sobbing. My dad hadn't ever been an emotional guy, but he started crying so hard he had to pull over to the side of the road. He put his hand on my shoulder and said, "I wish it was me, Paul." He also said that he had called Dr. Kern from the car while I was in the lab and asked if he could donate one of his testicles, but he was told that wasn't an option. The memory of that car ride is still so vivid to me. I don't remember ever feeling so close to my dad.

Ten seconds after we arrived, my mom and dad and I were all crying and hugging in the kitchen. They told me, "We're not going to let anything happen to you. We'll protect you." I knew that they knew that keeping those promises was beyond their control, but it meant the world to me that they said them. I always knew that they loved me, but that was the first time they had expressed their love for me in such an emotional way. From that day forward, our relationship was deeper, more powerful, and more meaningful.

The next morning, November 2, 1989, as I was being prepared for surgery, I was trying not to freak out. My mom had a lot of surgeries when I was a kid and all I remembered was seeing her out cold in a hospital bed with tubes and monitors everywhere. I was so fearful of being put under that they gave me a spinal block instead and draped my chest area so I couldn't see what was going on during the procedure. The drugs they gave me had made me a little loopy but I remember the doctor saying, "Well, we're going to get started. How do you feel, Paul?" I couldn't feel the whole bottom half of my body so I thought my legs were floating in the air. I said, "I think I'm good, but will you put my feet back down on the table?" The doctor chuckled and said, "I think he's ready."

When I woke up in the recovery room, I learned that even though it had been a small tumor I would need to start radiation treatment soon: one session every day for a month. Maybe it was because I was a young, healthy guy but I hardly reacted to the radiation. I'd see other patients who started the treatment at the same time I did end up in wheelchairs after just a few days. In fact, some of them stopped showing up at all. I was beginning to feel a little guilty so I asked the nurse, "Hey, are you sure you're radiating me? Because I'm not feeling anything. And I was out last night until 2 AM." They said, "Yes, you're just responding really well to it." I still felt guilty, but also very lucky and grateful.

I have kind of a silly character so the way I overcame the emotional trauma of having cancer and radiation was to be upbeat and happy-go-lucky and try to coax some laughs out of the nurses. During my treatments, I had to lie naked on the table so I'd do stupid little things like tie a ribbon around my penis or use lipstick to write some scrambled-up letters on my stomach and say, "Can you guess the word of the day?" They loved it. I did anything I could to lighten up the mood. On my last day of treatment, the medical staff had a little party for me and told me, "We're going to miss you, Paul. You've been so inspirational and you're such a beautiful person." It really made me feel special. I smiled and said, "I'm going to miss you too, but I hope I never have to see you again!"

That was wishful thinking on my part. A year after my surgery, I was at a Halloween party for American Airlines employees in Dallas. A pilot had rented out an entire roller-skating rink for all the employees and it was a blast. Suddenly, I felt a weird sick sense come over me. I turned to Janice and said, "I'm sick again." She said, "What do you mean? You have a cold?" "I told her, "No, I have cancer again." She tried to brush my fears away: "No, you don't. You're fine." I said, "No, we've gotta go."

I had no symptoms whatsoever, but the next morning, I called Dr. Kern's office, then hopped on a plane and flew to Minnesota for an ultrasound. Sure enough, Dr. Kern looked at the films in disbelief and said, "I've never seen this before. You have a tumor now in your left side." He told me that when someone has cancer in both testicles, it usually spreads to the other organs, but because I caught both cancers in the earliest stages, I had a much better chance of surgically removing it all and making a full recovery. He said he'd get me scheduled for surgery the next day and asked if I wanted another fake testicle. I was feeling pretty down and for some reason I said no. But I was still thinking clearly enough to head back to the cryogenic lab and leave another sample, although it turned out to be a waste of time because I later found out that my earlier radiation treatment had made me completely sterile.

After the surgery, I went back to my parent's house to recuperate. Since I could potentially still have children thanks to my first sperm bank deposit, I had pretty much come to terms with being sterile. But I was pretty emotional about having to go through radiation or chemo again, even though I had made it through treatment the first time without feeling sick. I dreaded having to put my whole life on hold for the second time in nine months.

The day after surgery, Dr. Kern called with some good news. He said he had been on a conference call about my case with specialists at the Mayo Clinic and from as far away as Europe. He told me that because I had been radiated before and because my type of cancer was pure seminoma instead of non-seminoma, I wouldn't need any follow-up treatment. I was stunned. I said, "I don't have to have chemo, radiation, nothing?" He said, "No." And I've been fine ever since.

I went back to flying again pretty quickly and was my old crazy self. I figured there was no reason to be shy about having had cancer, so I made light of it. I had always been a fun flight attendant. For example, Pee Wee Herman was really popular at the time and I would make announcements like,

"Please be sure your seat belt is fastened!" in a Pee Wee Herman voice. Lots of times when I did something goofy, a passenger would say, "You're nuts!" And I'd say, "No I'm not, I'm nut." They'd look at me weird like, "What are you talking about?" but the flight attendant on the other end of the cart would laugh because she knew that I only had one testicle. I'd be a liar if I told you that having cancer hadn't adversely impacted my life but my attitude was, *Hey, it happened, I'll grow and learn from it, but I won't let it get me down.*

I didn't realize it at the time but taking that approach ended up inspiring a lot of people. Shortly after I started dating a woman named Gia, for example, the subject of cancer came up. We got to talking and it turned out that she had spent five years in the hospital with cancer when she was a child. Her parents were told there was only a 1 percent chance she would survive. Later on, when we were in a relationship, Gia told me that I had inspired her. She said, "Your outlook with cancer was so different than mine. I felt guilty for living. I felt like I split up my parents." It felt good that talking about it with her helped her deal with those issues and relieve some of her pain. I knew I couldn't have shined any light on her suffering if I hadn't suffered myself.

A year later when Gia and I went on a cruise, she was sitting on the edge of the pool and I was standing in the shallow end, holding onto her knees as her legs dangled in the water. I said, "You know, I think I sabotaged a lot of relationships because I've always felt unworthy to have a wife. What woman would want to be with me when I can't give her children?" And she said to me, "That never occurred to me, Paul. I never thought that you were less of a man. If anything, you were more of a man to me for dealing with it so well."

Even though I think I handled my cancer scares pretty well, they definitely left their mark on me. Not being able to have kids has left a few dents in my self-image, but I'd say my reticence to get married is the biggest negative effect. I also have to get hormone shots every two weeks for the rest of my life. I do my best to be nonchalant about it, but every single time that needle goes in me I flash back to how terrified I was about dying so young. It's an awful reminder but I know it's only going to last a second and I'll be fine again.

Looking back though, I don't regret having had cancer. In fact, a lot of good has come out of it. It shaped the way I look at the world. Instead of complaining about my problems, I learned to make the most of what I've got every day. In a strange way, I didn't really start living until I thought I was dying. I had been suppressing a big chunk of my personality because of my fears and insecurities, but I decided pretty quickly that if I was going to have to check out, I was going to live each day to the fullest and not hold back anymore. That might mean bounding up on stage to sing karaoke instead of sitting shyly in the corner or just being more gregarious and outgoing around strangers.

In other words, surviving cancer gave me more guts. Later on, if I was making a sales call on a high-powered executive, sure, I'd be a little nervous, but I'd also think, *Screw that. I'm tougher than they are. They haven't been through what I've been through.* I not only had more drive, determination, and passion, I realized that those are the qualities that make people successful, not whether they got straight A's in high school.

Having to face the possibility of death at such a young age also made me more introspective. I started searching for more meaning and purpose in my life. Going deeper within made me discover a whole lot more about myself a whole lot sooner than I probably would have. Oh, I was still pretty clueless the rest of my twenties but at least I was aware that I didn't have a clue!

Most importantly, if I hadn't experienced what I did, I doubt that I would have realized that I'm here on the planet to help others any way I can and to inspire them to find the strength to make it through the tough times. I want to show people that they're more resilient and resourceful than they ever thought possible, and that not only can they survive, they can triumph over adversity even in the darkest of times.

Conquering Cancer
Your Life, Your Thoughts

- If you have ever come face to face with your own mortality, how did your perspective change as a result?

- How has a personal crisis affected your relationships with the people you loved most?

- In your moments of greatest vulnerability, what did you learn about yourself?

- What emotional scars do you still carry as a result of a past crisis and how do they affect your self-image and the quality of your daily life?

- Although a crisis of any kind is devastating at the time, what blessings have come out of your most challenging experiences?

- In what ways have your greatest challenges enabled you to help others who are going through difficult times of their own?

- In your hour of greatest need, who are the people you know you can turn to for help and support?

RIPPED OFF IN RIO

After eight years as a flight attendant based out of Dallas/Fort Worth International, I changed my home base to Miami International for two reasons: I qualified for seniority in Miami and I wanted to go to Central and South America, destinations that Dallas didn't fly to. I still lived in Dallas so if I had a flight scheduled, I'd fly into Miami, take a trip for a few days, then fly home for four days off. Working out of Miami was awesome; over the first six weeks I went on four three-day trips with the same sixteen-person crew. They were young and cool and we had a blast together.

In 1995, a year after I transitioned to Miami, our crew worked a flight to Brazil and laid over at a beautiful hotel in Rio de Janeiro. It felt like I was vacationing more than working. A bunch of us were lying around the big hotel pool, soaking up the sun, when the captain said, "We're all going out for some great Brazilian steak tonight. My treat. And after dinner, we'll check out a club." I said, "Great! I'm in." Four other crew members jumped in too. The six of us piled into a van and were dropped off at a Brazilian steakhouse in a central square filled with restaurants and shops. We had an incredible meal; everyone was talking and laughing and having a great time. After flying internationally for more than a year, I still found myself looking around fairly often, thinking, *Man, what a life!* Whether it was Madrid, Paris, or Rio de Janeiro, I was working with cool people and having the time of my life.

After dinner, we found a great disco for drinks and dancing. Around one in the morning, the captain said we'd better wrap it up so we went outside and flagged down a couple of taxis. I ended up with the captain and another flight attendant in the taxi in front. On the way back to the hotel, which was on the other side of a mountain from where we were, I noticed that we weren't going back the same way we came. Instead of taking the major highway, we took a mountain pass back. It was a gorgeous view, with the Rio de Janeiro skyline behind us and the Atlantic Ocean reflecting the city lights to our left.

Suddenly, we were slowing down and stopping. There looked to be a military vehicle on the side of the road. When I saw a uniformed man with a machine gun standing in the road, my first thought was that it was a military checkpoint, which is not uncommon in certain foreign countries. I wasn't too concerned until our taxi driver started arguing with the military guy. Something about their rapid-fire discussion and exaggerated hand gestures seemed a bit staged. I nudged the captain and whispered, "I think we're being robbed." Sure enough, the taxi driver turned to us a minute later and said in English, "You must give him all your goods." Even though we half-expected it, we just stared at him, unblinking, like, *Are you kidding me? This can't be happening.* The driver added, "You must give him everything or you go to jail." When the military guy poked his gun in the window, we knew we had zero options. Either we did what they asked or we'd be in big trouble.

Somewhere during my transition from surreal to terrified, I remembered the bulletins put out by American Airlines warning employees about potentially dangerous encounters and situations when traveling internationally. At the top of the list of do's and don'ts was an alert about never wearing expensive jewelry on layovers. That never concerned me because I didn't have much money or anything of value to worry about. But the captain was wearing a Rolex—the operative word being *was*. The other flight attendant riding with us lost her wedding ring and necklace. His wallet and her purse were also seized. When my turn came, I offered the guy my Iron Man watch but he wasn't interested. I opened up my wallet and all I had was my driver's license and three dollars. He gave me a dirty look and let me keep it. At the same time we were getting ripped off, another military guy with a gun was relieving the other three members of our crew of their valuables. Finally, the gun guys waved us on and we drove off.

Once we hit the main road where there were lights and lots of traffic, the captain told the driver to pull over; he got out and walked back to the other taxi to make sure everyone there was all right. The taxi driver apologized and said how badly he felt but we didn't feel like talking; it was a quiet ride back.

As soon as we got back to the hotel, the captain alerted hotel management, who summoned security. They quickly converged on the taxi driver; he pleaded ignorance but security was on to him. It turns out this scam had happened before and they were certain the driver was in on it but couldn't prove it. It almost sounded like they were giving him a scolding. I don't know what, if anything, ended up happening to the driver. I was just glad to be alive. The robbery itself was scary but we were probably more shaken up when it finally sunk in that we could have been kidnapped or killed. That's when it struck me that another airline bulletin had cautioned us to be aware of scams that were designed to take advantage of our helplessness in certain situations, particularly ones involving the police and other authorities. It made perfect sense: What better time to rip off tourists than late at night when they were vulnerable and a little tipsy. The taxi driver takes a different route back on a dark, secluded road. Everybody gets scared, nobody gets hurt, the taxi driver claims innocence, and the bad guys get away with the loot. It's genius, actually.

Once security had assumed command and we were no longer needed, the six of us retreated to the hotel bar. We were all still in shock a bit and needed to process what we had been through. Even though it was late, nobody wanted to go back to their room and be alone. The captain told us to order whatever we wanted and put it on his tab, and we were happy just to drink ourselves past the point of caring.

Needless to say, getting ripped off in the mountains of Brazil was a huge wake-up call. Glancing at a bullet point in a memo doesn't have quite the same impact as having actual bullets pointed at your head. I'm a lot more cautious today than I would have been had that robbery never occurred. Now, whenever I get into a taxi in a foreign country, I make sure it's well-marked, I make a note of the driver's name and number, and I interact with him to establish a certain degree of comfort. While I feel badly that my coworkers lost wedding rings, watches, and other expensive jewelry, all I lost was my naïveté. And that's not necessarily a bad thing.

Ripped Off In Rio
Your Life, Your Thoughts

- What are three things you can do to keep your awareness high when you're traveling internationally or domestically?

- What are three things you can do to protect yourself and your belongings when you feel vulnerable in an unfamiliar environment?

CASINO CON GAME

In February 2004, my girlfriend Krissy and I flew to Puerta Plata in the Dominican Republic with my best friend Tim Mieczkowski and his wife Lovette for a weeklong winter vacation. I knew Puerta Plata would be the perfect resort because I'd been there frequently as a flight attendant. The four of us were close and enjoyed each other's company. After a few days, Krissy and Lovette announced that they were going to do some fun "girl things" that night. That was fine with Tim and me; we headed to the bar for a few drinks and then walked over to the nearby casino.

A few minutes after Tim and I entered the casino, we were offered a free roll at a table game called Progressive Roulette. Neither of us had heard of it but it sure looked cool: You threw red balls into a round bowl that was filled with holes numbered one to six. The balls would settle into holes, the dealer would add up your points, and you'd see how close you were getting to a monster payout. Tim and I threw some money down, took a few turns, and started piling up points like we were pinball wizards. Every point they awarded us was catnip; once we got rolling, we couldn't stop. The dealer kept selling us hard. He told us that NBA star Charles Barkley had been there a month earlier and had walked out with over a hundred grand. "It's the person who stays in the game who wins," we were told. "Everyone quits too early because they don't have enough money." Our egos took that as a challenge and we kept those balls moving fast and furious. We were so close to the grand prize, we could almost taste the champagne we'd be celebrating with. Then just like that, our smoking hot luck turned ice cold. Foolishly, I ignored the alarm bells ringing in my head for a few more throws. After repeatedly coming up empty, I managed to shake my gambling jones long enough to say, "Hey, Tim, we better check and see how much money we owe." We each had about a thousand bucks on us, so I asked the dealer how much we were down. He wouldn't tell us, and kept encouraging us to keep playing. Finally, I said, 'No! Were done. What do we owe?"

As soon as the words left my mouth, a tough-looking pit boss with a New York accent and an expensive suit was at our side, flanked by two more mafioso-type guys. After we handed over all our cash, the pit boss amicably informed us that we owed another $3,500. Tim and I gulped hard. Trying to stay calm, I said, "Our ATM cards don't go up

that high; we can only get $500 a day from them."
The pit boss politely but firmly said, "Why don't
you come in the back room with us?" I could tell
by the look on Tim's face that he was thinking the
same thing I was: *Oh, crap, I've seen this movie before.*
Our next thoughts were, *Well, we don't have a choice
and I'm pretty sure we're not going to be murdered,* so we
meekly followed them through a back door. The pit
boss was all business. He asked if we had any credit
cards with us. I started sweating because mine were
all maxed out. Tim volunteered a card but when it
got declined, the mood in the room turned a whole
lot more serious. Tim used the casino's phone to call
the credit card company and found out the charge
was rejected because the company was suspicious
about a large payment at a gambling institution in
the Dominican Republic. Tim assured the company
that the charge was legit but they refused to approve
it. If this had been a movie, the background music
would have gotten louder and more dramatic. Shak-
ing a bit, Tim handed over a second card and, thank
God, that one went through.

As we slunk out of the casino, I told Tim,
"Don't worry, as soon as we get back, I'll give you
my portion of it." All Tim said was, "We can't ever,
ever tell anybody about this. I am so embarrassed." I
agreed and we made a pact not to tell a soul. Luckily,
Krissy's insistence on paying half of our expenses
helped me camouflage my lack of available cash the
rest of the trip.

Over the years, Tim and I would laugh about
the incident to ourselves, but nobody else ever

knew, not even Krissy and Lovette. Our casino caper would've stayed between us had Tim not insisted that I include the story in this book. Just thinking about Krissy reading this makes me wince a bit but I'm sure she'll get a good laugh out of it.

Eight years later, I still shake my head over how Tim and I allowed ourselves to get suckered so badly. It was little consolation to learn that the Internet is bulging with stories about people who got scammed with Progressive Roulette at Dominican casinos. As stupid as we were that night, we're smarter than that. We understood casinos. I did a lot of business in Vegas and Tim was great with numbers and odds. But we got swept up in the moment, got seduced way too easily, and started gambling with money we couldn't afford to lose. If I ran my business like that—believing I was bulletproof and could ignore reality—I'd be panhandling in no time. It was a tough lesson to learn but I'm actually glad it happened when it did. If I had been in that casino just a few years later after selling my company for millions, I may have kept rolling those damn balls until I lost a helluva lot more than I did. Sorry, Gordon Gekko, greed is *not* good.

Casino Con Game
Your Life, Your Thoughts

- Given that drinking and gambling is a combination that can get you into real trouble real quickly, what can you do to minimize your risk of being taken advantage of?

- If you found yourself in a financial emergency in a foreign country, how could you arrange to have access to extra cash?

- When traveling outside of the United States, why is it a good idea to remind yourself that you're not protected by the U.S. legal system?

SECTION IV

FRIENDS AND LOVERS

*As an incurable romantic, I see all of life
as a romance. My most intimate relationships have
given me invaluable insights into myself
and into life itself.*

FRIENDS FIRST
AND FOREVER

I had just returned home from a flight to Paris in October 1990 on FIberNev business when Janice, the woman I was living with, asked me if she could use my truck. I said, "Of course you can. Why? Did you buy something?" She said, "No, I rented an apartment, I'm moving out tomorrow." I blurted out, "You are?" She said, "Paul, we've been dating for five years. I love you, I care about you, but I'm ready to settle down and get married and I don't see that happening with you. I see you going through a lot of life discovery; I applaud you for it and I don't hold anything against you. We're just in two different places."

Janice was right. I had a lot of soul-searching yet to do. My cancer diagnosis had triggered a reexamination of my whole life, and I knew I wasn't yet the person I wanted to be. Janice was a fantastic woman and I didn't want to break up with her, but it was obvious that she wanted more from me than I could give her at the time. Even as we were going our separate ways, I couldn't help but respect and appreciate the honest, straightforward way she went about it. After I got over the initial shock of her announcement, I actually felt relieved because I was once again free to explore life in whatever direction it took me. If there's a textbook case of how to end a relationship in a healthy, mutually beneficial way, this was it. There was zero animosity or arguing. I even helped Janice move.

Before Janice had announced she was leaving, we had booked a five-day cruise for January with a bunch of our mutual friends. I assumed we'd cancel the reservation or that Janice would go on the cruise with the guy she had started dating shortly after we split up. To my surprise, she told me that her new boyfriend was okay with us going on the cruise together with our friends. I remember thinking, *Wow, what a guy. He must really be trusting.* It made perfect sense that Janice would be with someone like that because she was very trustworthy herself.

The day of the cruise, I picked Janice up at her apartment for our flight to Miami. It was great to see her again. She had never looked better and the thought crossed my mind that breaking up may have been a mistake. But that thought was quickly followed by the realization that even though I still loved Janice, I wasn't in love with her romantically and hadn't been for quite some time. Even so, it had taken a while to heal from losing her. I had missed her love and companionship.

The cruise was wonderful and memorable, but not at all in the way I would have expected. On the second day, Janice got seasick and I was at her side the rest of the day taking care of her. It felt like the most natural thing in the world to stay with her in our room, bring her chicken soup, and nurse her back to health. Later that day, as I was caring for her, Janice looked at me and said, "You know Paul, I love you so much." It was a magical moment. Feeling such unconditional love pouring from her made me feel so good. In no way was she suggesting that we get back together, it was simply an expression of unconditional love and gratitude between two people who shared an unbreakable bond of friendship. During the cruise, we kept our twin beds separate but I don't ever remember feeling closer to her.

Within a year after the cruise, Janice married her boyfriend. Eighteen years later, she's happily married with a family. I have no regrets whatsoever about our time together. During those five years, she was incredibly supportive as I dealt with the pain and trauma of having cancer. She also started and finished her four-year degree while working alongside me as a flight attendant. I don't know that either one of us could've done what we did without each other. I am still grateful for her friendship and her presence in my life.

Friends First And Forever
Your Life, Your Thoughts

- What has each of your relationships taught you about yourself, about relationships, and about life?

- Thinking back to the way previous relationships have ended, what regrets do you have and what do you wish you had done differently?

- If you've stayed in relationships that had run their course, what fears prevented you from ending them when the time was right?

- In what ways do you see your previous relationships as successes instead of failures?

MAGIC IN MADRID

Transferring my home base from Dallas/Fort Worth International Airport to Miami International Airport was one of the best moves I ever made. I was single and having the time of my life. But after not dating anyone regularly for three or four months, I was ready for some romance.

The first night of a European trip, we had a lay over in Madrid. After getting settled in my room, I went down to the hotel lobby to meet the crew for a drink like we normally did. The two pilots were already down there and we hit it off well. I was telling them about my adventures in the fiber optic lighting business when Mandy, a flight attendant I had been flirting with, arrived. She came over, gave me a hug, and said to the pilots, "Wouldn't we make beautiful children together?" That got my attention, because a girl doesn't say that about a guy unless she's interested. The rest of the crew started filtering in, and when everyone was there, we set off for dinner, drinks, and sightseeing.

The captain led us to Plaza Mayor in Madrid, which by definition means "the major plaza." Nowadays, it's a gathering spot and a tourist attraction ringed by shops and cafes, but in decades and centuries past, it was the site of bullfights, soccer games, and even public executions. Our first stop was a tapas bar, which is essentially a restaurant that serves only appetizers. I felt like I was in a dream; here I was, a Minnesota boy with stars in his eyes, drinking wine in Madrid with fifteen cool coworkers, listening to Spanish music, flirting with a cute girl, and gaping at the dramatic paintings and photos of bullfighting that lined the walls. I couldn't believe how lucky I was to be there and experience it all.

When the captain said, "Let's go to dinner," we enthusiastically agreed. We walked over toward some large, really old buildings that looked like they were carved out of rock. The one we went into housed a restaurant that the servers told us Hemingway used to frequent. It reminded me of a big pub, with live music and a bar and everyone having a good time. The energy there was fantastic.

Toward the end of the meal, I excused myself to go to the bathroom. Mandy said, "I need to go too; I'll go with you." I asked a server where the men's room was and she pointed toward a steep, narrow staircase that spiraled downward into darkness. The stairs looked they were carved out of dirt and rocks and it felt like we were descending into the bowels of the earth. What was really cool was that there were light-filled spaces carved into the side of the walls for intimate gatherings or romantic private settings. We passed one space near the bottom where four guys were passing around a jug of wine and playing flamenco music. After visiting the bathroom, I was waiting for Mandy to come out when the musicians waved me over. I walked over and sat down on an overturned bucket like the ones they were sitting on. It was dark, I had a wine buzz, and their music was pulling me in and swallowing me up. Mandy came out, walked over, sat in my lap, and put her arms around me. We never went back upstairs. We just listened to the music with our arms wrapped around each other. It felt like the songs they were playing transported us to another dimension where our souls pulsated in time with the music.

After what seemed like a couple of hours, the captain came downstairs looking for Mandy and me. He was relieved we were okay and asked what we were doing. "We're being serenaded," I told him happily. When he said the rest of the group was getting ready to leave, I told him, "Okay, no problem, we'll find our way back." It was just too wonderful of an evening to leave before we had to; neither of us was ready for the night to end. We stayed another hour or so, soaking up the atmosphere, drinking wine, and munching on chips. The longer we sat there, the closer I felt to Mandy. By the time the musicians called it a night, I felt like I had known her for years. We were both pretty hammered by the time we got back to the hotel. Neither of us said a word; we just went straight to her room and fell into bed.

In the morning, I woke up with a start. Somebody was pounding on the door. I threw on a pair of pants and opened the door. It was the captain. I didn't have to explain anything. I was in her room and he knew it. He said, "We're all down in the airport limo ready to go. You're late." Boy, was that a wake-up call! I woke up Mandy and we scrambled to get ready. I think we were still buttoning up our uniforms in the elevator. We jumped onto the bus and got a standing ovation from the rest of the crew. Mandy and I both felt pretty sheepish but we played along and bowed to our adoring fans. Still, it was pretty embarrassing.

When we got back to Miami, we all said our goodbyes and scattered like we always did. I didn't speak to Mandy again until five days later, when it was time to do the same trip again. She brought it up first: "You know, Paul, I . . . we probably did a little too much." I said, "Yeah, we probably did, but you know what? I wouldn't change a thing." She smiled and said, "I wouldn't either. But I think I'm just going to lay low tonight." "Hey, no problem," I told her. We both understood that it had been a one-time thing and neither of us mentioned it again.

It's been almost twenty years, but whenever I think back to that night with Mandy, I can't help but smile. It was the most intensely romantic experience of my life. It was a beautiful evening that made me feel very special, which is something I needed at the time; and I think Mandy needed it too. What's especially cool is that it didn't take place in a traditional romantic setting like an expensive restaurant or a five-star hotel; it was just the two of us sitting on a bucket in a rocky cave. And it couldn't have been more perfect.

What that night with Mandy helped me realize is that we can get so wrapped up in past events or future expectations that we can fail to recognize a magical moment when it's ours for the taking. I will always be grateful that we seized the moment, and I'll never give up hope that someday I can experience that feeling again.

Magic In Madrid
Your Life, Your Thoughts

- How have your views on romance evolved over the years?

- What have your most romantic experiences taught you about life and love?

- What can you do right now to set a romantic adventure in motion?

LOVING LILIANA

After exiting TexGlow in 1992, I took a year off from the fiber optic business to lick my wounds and figure out what I wanted to do next. During that hiatus, I became friends with Keith, a successful, sharp-dressed guy with a fun personality who invited me to join his business. Keith helped people repair their credit and establish better credit ratings. I thought that sounded pretty cool so I told him I'd help him out on my days off from flying.

For the first couple of weeks I shadowed Keith to see exactly what he did and to look for opportunities to make myself indispensable. It didn't take long for me to realize that he was a master at smoke and mirrors. His spiel sounded good, but the way I saw it, he was taking advantage of low-income people with poor credit by charging them a fee to work with credit bureaus on their behalf and help them obtain a secured credit card. His customers didn't realize that this was something they could do for themselves. Granted, some people would rather pay someone else for services like this but I thought Keith was preying on their ignorance. Even so, I kept showing up because the technical side of the business fascinated me. I ended up learning a lot about fixing bad credit, and to this day I still help people out with that whenever I can.

Although I rapidly lost interest in working with Keith, I felt increasingly drawn to Liliana, the beautiful young woman who did all the prospecting for the company. It didn't take long for me to become smitten. We flirted a bit, and even had a few nice lunch dates, but nothing that I would call romantic. As I got to know her, I learned that she was seeing a guy but that it didn't seem to be working. When she told me they had broken up, I thought, *Now's my chance.*

Just a few days later, I asked Keith where Liliana was. He shrugged and said she hadn't shown up for work. The next day, she was a no-show again. She finally called that afternoon . . . from jail. She told us that she had been getting government assistance for the past few months and hadn't told the county that she had found a job, so she was arrested for double-dipping. She had a court date in two days and was hoping to get on work release, so she asked if we would write a letter to the judge. I told her I absolutely would write a letter on her behalf because she did a great job for us and was valuable to the company. I took the letter to the courthouse on the day of her hearing, and as I watched the proceedings, I remember thinking how beautiful she was even in an orange jumpsuit. I realized I was falling for her, which was weird, because I really didn't know her that well, and besides, she was in jail.

The judge looked to be a cowboy type in his early sixties, like he had just come from the ranch after roping a few steers. When he asked me for the letter, he asked me to say a few words too, which I did. Not that it did any good. The judge harrumphed that he didn't care what Liliana did for us, that she was a menace to society and needed to be locked up for six months. I was shocked. Liliana's attorney later told me that the judge didn't like minorities, which I had figured out pretty quickly. Throwing Liliana in jail just didn't make any sense. It was going to cost the government more money to keep her in jail than what it had paid her in assistance. Why not just make her pay restitution? Besides, she had two little kids who needed their mom. I decided on the spot that I would help her out. For better or worse, when I value and care about somebody, I don't judge what they did; I just feel compelled to do what I can to help.

Over the next six months, Liliana and I exchanged phone calls and letters and I managed to see her almost every day, even if it was just for a few seconds. She was in a jail that had been converted from an old hotel. It was right off the freeway heading to Dallas, so she would go to a window, even though it had bars around it, and wave to me as I drove by. As the weeks and months went by, the more I couldn't be with her the more I wanted to be with her and I'd visit her whenever I could. I remember being surprised that she'd have makeup on. She laughed and said, no, they didn't give the inmates makeup; the prostitutes there showed her how to scrape the color from the ink in magazines to make eye shadow and other types of makeup. Talk about resourceful! I'm no fashion expert but she looked like she had been worked on by a professional makeup artist. I liked that she had gone to the trouble to make herself look nice for me. We enjoyed flirting with each other and it felt like a nice relationship was developing. We were both looking forward to the day she'd be released from jail.

On the afternoon that Liliana was released I picked her up at the jail and brought her to her sister's apartment, where her kids had been living for the past six months. The kids were spending the night with their father, but a handful of her relatives were there, waiting to welcome her. Liliana's family was very close so it was fun for me to be there and celebrate with them. It was challenging too; the Spanish was flying fast and furious and I could only catch a word here and there.

It was a week night so Liliana's parents and other sister headed home shortly after dark so they could get up early for work. We stayed up talking to her sister and brother-in-law for a bit, and then were left on the couch in the living room when they went to bed. After six months of longing, all it took was one look from Liliana and we were in each other's arms, sharing our first kiss. It was wonderful to actually be holding her; she suggested taking it further, but I stopped after ten minutes and told her that I wanted our first time to be more special and romantic. I drove home feeling happy about the night and excited about what was to come.

It took a few weeks for Liliana to ease back into the rhythm of a normal life. She moved in with her parents for a while and spent time reconnecting with her children. Nate was five and Graciella was just two; they had different fathers but Graciella's biological father shared some of the parenting duties for both the kids.

Liliana and I started dating, and within six months, she and her kids moved in with me. I was thrilled to have them there. I had been living all by myself in a three-bedroom townhouse and thought I was years away from having the wife and kids I wanted so much, and here I was with a beautiful woman who came with a ready-made family. I loved her, I loved her kids. It was perfect.

I really enjoyed growing into being a father fig-ure for Nate and Graciella. I'd take Graciella to dance classes and teach Nate how to work on cars, but the main thing I did for them was just to be there and love them. I had always wanted kids so I could pass on the unconditional love and caring that I got from my parents. It was satisfying to know that my spending time with them and developing a strong emotional bond would have a lasting effect and play a significant role in how they felt about themselves.

Even though I felt like I had stepped into a *Leave It to Beaver* episode, I still wrestled with my doubts and insecurities. Liliana was a good person but her lapses in integrity nagged at me occasionally. I'd ask myself, *What am I doing with a woman who'd been in jail?* Plus, I may not have admitted it back then but I was still beating myself up about my inability to have children organically and questioning whether I was worthy of an emotionally healthy, self-sufficient woman. I ended up rationalizing that being with Liliana and her kids was a gift from God, a way of making lemonade out of lemons for both of us. It felt like we were supposed to be together and that being a dad to Nate and Graciella was my calling.

I was a good influence on Liliana. I encouraged her to make the most of her skills and develop her self-confidence. For instance, she spoke Portuguese and Spanish, but after getting out of jail, she was working a dead-end job for eight bucks an hour. I told her, "Liliana, you're a smart person. Why don't you get out of retail and go work for a bigger company that can utilize your language skills?" After some searching, I found a job posting for an oil-and-gas company. They were looking for an office assistant who spoke Spanish and Portuguese. I thought, *Wow, this is perfect.* Liliana's initial reaction was that she could never land such a great job, but I knew she'd wow them if she dressed up and demonstrated her language skills. I bought her a nice outfit for the interview and, sure enough, she was hired on the spot for forty-five grand a year, as much as I was making. The last piece of my happiness puzzle had fallen into place: Liliana was doing fulfilling, enjoyable work that paid well. It was a great life.

A little more than a year after we had officially started dating, Liliana and I drove eight hours south of Dallas to meet her parents the week after Christmas. They were from Monterey, Mexico, but were now living in McAllen, Texas. They were lovely, hard-working people and very family oriented. Liliana had five brothers and sisters and they were all meeting at their parents' house to celebrate the holidays.

I remember being outside with her dad, who loved to grill. We were trying to have a conversation while he was tending to his grilling, but it was a bit awkward because he didn't speak English well and I kept having to ask him to repeat everything. Then, out of nowhere, he looked at me and said, "Paul you are a good man. Why my daughter Liliana? She will hurt you. She still needs to figure out what is important in life. And you know what is important. You are a great man; I'm proud she would be with a man like you. But be careful. You are going to get hurt."

I was shocked. As he was telling me this, I was thinking, *How could you possibly say these things about your own daughter?* He struck me as a good man, but he knew nothing about me and had just met me for the first time. That night, as I lay in a single bed in a little room in their home, I thought hard about what he had told me. I concluded that he was telling me that he loved his daughter but that he knew she had some shortcomings she needed to work on. He was a proud man and I could tell it bothered him to think of anyone making his name look bad. In effect, he was saying, "If she betrays you, that's like me betraying you, and I am an honorable man." I couldn't do anything but respect that.

The next morning, I heard Liliana's mom bustling about in the kitchen at four o'clock, hand-making tortillas. By seven thirty, all of us were crammed into a little room off the kitchen, eating a wonderful homemade Mexican breakfast. Near the end of the meal, Liliana's dad said, "Paul, so you tell me, my wife wants to know, what do you want for lunch? What you say, she will make." People were still a little chatty, but they all wanted to hear what I was going to say because whatever I decided is what they were also going to have for lunch. At first I thought, *Wow, that's a lot of pressure.* After all, I had just met most of these people and I wasn't familiar with their preferences. Then I relaxed and thought, *You know what, these people are my family now so it would be cool to announce my choice in Spanish.* With a big smile, I said, "Chupa!"

Have you ever wondered what it would be like to snap your fingers and have everyone in the room freeze in position? Well, I don't have to wonder any more. Liliana's mom, who had been standing up while mixing something in a bowl, was rooted to the spot, staring at me in disbelief. Everyone else was a statue too, their eyes bulging out. I was confused. "What? What?" I said feebly. Then Liliana blurted out something in Spanish and everyone started laughing.

Liliana then explained to me that chupa meant "sucks," and that even though there's a lollipop called a Chupa Pop, when a male says "chupa" to a female, it's essentially a request for, well, oral sex. Boy, did I feel cheap. Everyone started laughing again when I sheepishly explained that I was trying to order soup. Although I felt humbled and humiliated, I was glad that the moment had happened; everyone thought that my mistaking "chupa" for "sopa" was endearing. They all let their guard down and relaxed, and I felt like I had been welcomed into the family.

My life with Liliana and the kids was everything I had hoped for . . . until Thanksgiving the following year when I answered the phone. A male voice said, "Oh, hi. I was looking for Liliana. I just wanted to wish her a happy Thanksgiving." I said, "Sure, she's right here," and handed the phone to her. I didn't think anything of it, until the look on Liliana's face said it all. When she hung up, I asked her who the guy was. She said, "Oh, it's just a UPS guy that comes to the office. I gave him my number because his kids are friends with my kids." I said, "Oh, okay, no big deal." But the sick feeling in the pit of my stomach told me otherwise.

In the weeks that followed, I tried to give Liliana the benefit of the doubt but something just didn't seem right. She started going out with her girlfriends a little more often. Then one night, she came home tipsy. She ducked in the bathroom, then came straight to bed. I leaned over to give her a kiss and saw that she hadn't taken her makeup off. Her lipstick was all smudged and there was a hickey on her neck. My heart sank. I asked her what the hell was going on but she denied doing anything wrong. It was late, I was tired, and I was angry. I said, "Fine, we'll talk in the morning," and rolled over. The next day, she stuck to her story, which made me angrier because I knew she was lying. I finally told her we were through, that I couldn't live with a woman who wasn't honest with me. I temporarily moved in with a friend of mine until I could work through my emotions and figure out what to do next. I let Liliana stay in the townhouse because I loved her kids and didn't have the heart to uproot them again.

The next few weeks were hell. I loved Liliana and was grieving the loss of the family I had wanted so badly. She continued to proclaim her innocence until one day when we managed to set aside the anger and defensiveness. We had a heart-to-heart conversation about what we meant to each other and what a colossal loss breaking up would be. In a vulnerable moment, she broke down and admitted that she had indeed been with another guy. Her tears were genuine and she promised me it would never happen again. I wanted to believe her so badly that I accepted her apology and her promise. Was I naïve? Definitely. But I brushed aside the red flags and talked myself into trusting her again. I rationalized that because she had come so close to losing something so good, she would never go down that road again.

With a newfound understanding and a deeper sense of intimacy between us, we got back on track. Any misgivings I had about her indiscretion soon seemed like a distant memory. I was so convinced that Liliana was the love of my life that in the spring of '97, just a few months after nearly breaking up, I went all in. I flew my parents and her parents down to Dallas and took everyone to a nice restaurant. After dinner, during dessert, I got down on one knee and proposed with a custom-made diamond ring. She accepted. It was a wonderful moment. Finally, I would have the life I'd dreamed of with a wife and kids. My happiness was complete.

I proposed when I did because I wanted to make my intentions clear before I asked her to move to Minnesota with me. For the past few years, I had been helping my brother, Jerry, with Advanced Lighting, the company I had helped him start in 1993. I had been flying to Sauk Centre a couple of times a month, but business had picked up and I knew it was time to head back home and put everything I had into growing the business. Liliana, the kids, and I flew to Minnesota in May. We stayed at my parents' home for a few weeks until the lake home I bought was ready for us to move into.

Liliana was happy to make the move and she and the kids adapted well. Whenever she got a little homesick, we'd drive to a Mexican neighborhood or restaurant so she could enjoy being around other people who shared her cultural heritage. Graciella had no qualms at all about her new home. She knocked on all the neighbors' doors and said, "Hi, my name is Graciella. My dad is Paul. Do you have any candy?" Everyone just fell in love with her. One of my favorite memories from that time was camping across the lake with Nate, who was eight. We were in a tent, and I remember him looking up at me, his eyes shining, and asking, "Paul, is it okay if

I call you Dad all the time?" I smiled back and said, "Of course." What a great moment. Everything had come together just perfectly and I couldn't imagine how life could get any better.

Four months after moving to Minnesota, Liliana asked if I was okay with her flying back to Dallas to visit her family. I had expected that she'd want to go back two or three times a year, so I bought tickets for her and the kids and off they went. After a few hours, I called Liliana to make sure they had arrived safely but her cell phone was apparently off. Since she was going to be staying at her brother Miguel's house, I gave him a call. When he heard my voice on the phone, he said, "Hey, Paul, how's Liliana? I haven't talked to her in a while." In spite of the alarm bells going off in my head, I managed to say, "What? She's down there with you, isn't she?" Miguel said, "No, I haven't spoken to her in a couple of weeks. We were just going to call and see how you were doing." I stammered, "But . . . but she left to come be with you." I could hear the concern in Miguel's voice as he said, "Paul, she's not here." Stunned, I murmured "Oh, okay, bye," and hung up.

I felt like a mule had kicked me in the gut. I thought, *This can't be happening.* Then I caught myself. It *was* happening. And I had to find out what the hell was going on. The first thing I did was call her best friend in Dallas and ask if Liliana was there. She said, "No, her kids are with me but she went out with a friend." I thought, *Okay, that's a little weird. You're her best friend, why isn't she out with you?* Next, I pulled out our cell phone bill and zeroed in on an unfamiliar

Dallas-area number she had been calling a lot. By this time I was in detective mode and I came up with a plan: I would call the number at seven o'clock the next morning. If my suspicions were correct and she was with another man, they'd probably still be in bed and their guard would be down.

So early the next morning, I called. A guy answered. I said, very cheerfully, "Hey, how's it going? It's Paul. Can I talk to Liliana?" He said, "Sure," and handed the phone to her. I heard him tell her, "It's Paul," and she whispered back, "Paul? What? You're kidding me." She came on the phone, and I said, "Hey, Liliana. I just want to let you know that I know what you're up to, and it's bad enough what you're doing to me, but just think about what you're putting your kids through." And I hung up.

She called me back an hour later after she had a chance to get her bearings and come up with a story. She tried telling me that he was just a friend, but I said, "Liliana, you were in bed with him. I heard the covers moving when you rolled over." She continued to deny there was anything going on but I wasn't buying it and she knew it.

I hung up and found myself walking through the house, *our* house, with tears streaming down my face. There were Liliana's clothes, Nate and Graciella's toys, the swing set in the backyard I had built for the kids. It was a horrible day. And it wasn't going to get any easier because I knew I still had to see her and deal with all the logistics of them moving out. Worse yet was my grief over what would happen between the kids and me. Would I ever see them again? Would they hate me or judge me? I wanted to continue being a part of their lives but that was up to Liliana; it was completely out of my hands.

Finally, when Liliana got back to Minnesota, she opened up and told me the truth. I said, "Liliana, it's over. I can never trust you again. I did everything I could to give you a great life. I loved you, I loved your kids. I helped you get a great job and turn your life around. We moved across the country. If you weren't happy, you could have told me. But now you've caused all this pain, not only for me but also for your kids. It breaks my heart to say it but this is it, we're done."

A few days later, Liliana and the kids flew back to Texas for good. Saying goodbye to Nate and Graciella was gut-wrenching. I felt awful, not only because I had lost the woman I wanted to marry but also because I felt like I was abandoning the kids, which broke my heart into even more pieces. The next six months were miserable. I not only missed the kids and what I had with Liliana, I felt like I had lost *my family*, and that was the worst pain of all.

I made it a priority to stay in touch with Nate and Graciella. For the next few years, with Liliana's permission, I'd fly down fairly often and surprise the kids by picking them up after school. One day I waited outside the school for Graciella; when she came out and saw me, she jumped into my arms and said to her girlfriends who were waiting for the bus, "This is my favorite dad!" I was grateful that I could still be a positive presence in their lives. I even drove a brand-new Toyota Corolla down to Dallas and left it with Liliana for a year so she'd have safe, reliable transportation for the kids. As Nate and Graciella got older, I stayed in touch mostly via the phone. But then Liliana moved and I lost touch with them for a few years. By the time we had reestablished contact, the kids were teenagers and had lives of their own.

Fast-forward. It's twelve years after Liliana and I split up. The phone rings. It's Liliana, inviting me to Graciella's high school graduation party that Saturday. I tell her that I appreciate the invitation and that I will absolutely be there. Oh, and by the way, she tells me, she's divorcing the father of her third child, still has feelings for me, and could she borrow $1,500 for Graciella's graduation. She swears she'll be able to pay me back with the tax refund that's coming soon. I said sure and sent her a check. It was made out to Liliana but I was really giving it to Graciella, which I was happy to do.

Shortly after I landed in Dallas on Friday afternoon, Liliana called my cell. I made a point to tell her that, yes, I was in town but I was visiting with a bunch of old flight attendant friends. The next morning, as I drove up to the small house that Liliana was renting, a mature young man in his early twenties shouted, "Paul!" and gave me a hug when I got out of my rental car. He must have realized I didn't recognize him because he said, "It's Nate!" I said, "Oh, my God! You're all grown up!" He laughed and told me he was married with a couple of kids. As I stood there talking with Nate, the love I felt for him came flooding back into my heart as if no time had passed. It felt amazing to connect with him again.

I went inside and got a warm welcome from Liliana's family. Her parents started crying and told me how much they loved me and that they knew I was a great man. It was very humbling and touching to get all that love from them. Liliana's sisters were pretty much busting her chops for letting me get away, and she good-naturedly agreed. Being there made me realize how much I had missed being a part of such a family-oriented group of people. They were all about family, and I loved that.

From my years with Liliana, I knew that Mexican culture typically dictates that meat for a party is purchased right before it's to be cooked. So when Liliana mentioned she'd be right back with the seasoned meat, I told her I'd go with her. I figured it would be good for us to talk for a few minutes. She was fine with that, but told me that Johnny, Graciella's biological father, was also tagging along. I hesitated, because Johnny had always been somewhat of an absent father to Graciella; he was a railroad conductor and always traveling. So I had my preconceived notions about him and wondered if the outing was going to get confrontational. But he turned out to be warm and friendly and I liked him right away. He obviously had grown up and gotten his priorities in order. He was there for Graciella as she got older and was doing his best to make up for those lost early years. He paid for the meat and we drove back to the house.

I was glad to be at the party. We were all eating and laughing and having a good time. Liliana's nieces and nephews were giving me hugs and telling me how much they had missed me. After all these years I felt like I was part of the family again. When it came time to cut the cake, Graciella got up in front of everyone to say a few words. It was so good to see her again and to see what a lovely young woman she had become. She had been a straight-A student and was heading off to college soon. As she spoke of all the things she appreciated in her life, she said, "There's someone here who means more to me than anybody in the world. He is the one reason why I'm a good kid, a good student, and why I have goals in my life. He is my rock, he's my anchor. He hasn't been around a whole lot lately but he was there during the important times and was incredible." I was looking at Johnny and could see him getting emotional as Graciella spoke. I was happy that he had turned his life around and become a good father to his daughter. Then Graciella finished up by saying, "He's my favorite dad and I just want to say, 'Thank you, Paul.'" I was so surprised I was speechless. The tears started flowing and everyone else started crying and hugging me. It was a wonderful but surreal moment. I managed to make eye contact with Johnny and say, "Johnny, you're a good man. You're always going to be her father. It doesn't matter what happened in the past; all that matters is what you're doing now." He smiled, nodded, and shook my hand.

I was overcome with emotion. I gave Graciella a big hug and told her how proud I was of her. I hadn't realized I meant so much to her. Hearing those words from Graciella and feeling all the love from her and her family was worth all the emotional anguish I had endured from Liliana's lies and infidelity.

Yes, Liliana hurt me badly, but to be fair, she brought a lot of joy into my life as well. For a few years, our life together was magical and I feel lucky to have lived it. We had essentially been a married couple. We had it all. We went on romantic dates, threw big parties for family birthdays, went to the park with the kids. I loved doing with Liliana all the things that couples do together. I even loved grocery shopping with her. I really loved that life and thinking of it now makes me appreciate it all the more. Another thing that was tremendously gratifying was learning that I could love someone else's children as if they were my own. That was an amazing gift.

With the benefit of time and therapy, I can see how Liliana and I both contributed to the demise of the relationship. For my part, I knew before we got together that she had integrity issues. I mean, hello, she was in jail when I fell in love with her. I knew in my gut that I'd be better off with a woman who had everything together, who was trustworthy, responsible, and self-sufficient, but I rationalized my way into ignoring all the red flags that popped up around her. So that's on me.

Years after the fact, I talked about the end of our relationship with Liliana and she acknowledged that she had felt unworthy of being with a man like me who was smart and successful. How ironic is that? We had set ourselves up for failure and subconsciously sabotaged the relationship because we both felt undeserving of a healthy relationship. I am so grateful we revisited all this so I could get some answers about what happened and why. I had healed my grief about the relationship and had moved on, but hearing her side of the story helped me gain more closure and gave me a deeper measure of peace. It's such a shame that so many relationships end on a sour note with the former partners hardly communicating, much less patiently and honestly answering questions that could help each other heal.

What I took away from my relationship with Liliana was the resolve to keep my standards high and never again sell myself short. If I'm thinking about getting serious with a woman who appears to be lacking a quality that's important to me, it may or may not be a deal breaker but I'm going to address it with her right up front. It's a matter of staying true to my values and giving myself the best shot at a healthy, sustainable relationship.

Having said that, I'm glad I went forward with Liliana. Overall, spending four years with her was a great experience. I know now that the best way to learn about yourself is through relationships; but you're not going to have a genuinely fantastic relationship until you get to know yourself better. Ultimately, I have no regrets about being with her. I guess I just had to learn the hard way that not all fairy tales have happy endings.

Loving Liliana
Your Life, Your Thoughts

- How can rescuing someone from a difficult challenge of their own making be doing them a disservice?

- How have your romantic relationships reflected the state of your self-image at the time?

- How have you and a romantic partner dealt with each other's shortcomings and how could you have done a better job of doing so?

- In what ways have you rationalized away any red flags in your relationships and looked the other way rather than face potentially life-altering issues?

- If you've experienced betrayal by a partner, how has that experience changed your attitude and behavior in that relationship or in subsequent ones?

- What are the greatest gifts that have come out of your romantic relationships?

- In what ways, if any, have you unconsciously sabotaged your relationships because of self-worth issues?

- How have your previous relationships better prepared you for your subsequent relationships?

LOVE AND MONEY

I was riding down a mountain in a van with Bobby Kennedy, Jr. and others during the 2008 Deer Valley Celebrity Skifest in Utah. After meeting Bobby at Tom Gegax's house fourteen months earlier, he had invited me for the second year running to attend this Waterkeeper Alliance event and I was honored to be there. As we were returning from our gala dinner on top of the mountain, someone asked, "So how are you doing?" Cheerfully, I said, "I'm doing great, even though I just got an e-mail this morning from my boss confirming that I've been terminated." Bobby said, "Whoa, what happened?" I told him, "Well, you know I merged my company with a public company. When the economy went to hell, the board of directors decided somebody had to go and I was the highest-paid employee. But that's okay. It was all very respectful, we negotiated a separation package, and I think it'll turn out to be a win-win."

Bobby and others told me they were sorry to hear the news, but I was upbeat about it. I was already thinking about new businesses I could start. That led into a quick discussion of other adversities we had faced and overcome.

After the van dropped us off at the next event, I found myself talking to Gia, a lovely young woman who had been riding in the back of the van. Gia was the guest of a friend of hers who was the personal assistant to John Paul DeJoria, the billionaire co-founder of Paul Mitchell, the hair products company. I found out later that Gia had overheard me talking about losing my job and having cancer twice and thought, "Wow, I've got to get to know this guy. He's got a good, positive outlook on life." I'm glad she took the initiative because we really hit it off. A couple nights later, Gia, her friend, and I went out, danced a lot, and had a great time. Before we left Utah, we friended each other on Facebook and said we'd keep in touch.

That was in December. Over the next few months, we called and Facebooked each other. I was looking forward to an April business trip that would bring me to San Diego because Gia accepted my invitation to drive down from L.A. for dinner. When she told me she had to cancel because of a scheduling conflict, I said, "Listen, I'm going to New York for three days and then I'm going to my condo in Florida for four or five days. Why don't you meet me? You can have your own room and your own space. It'll be fun." She said she hadn't done anything like that before, but joked that since I knew

Bobby Kennedy, Jr., I must be a good guy. When she flew into New York, I hired a car to pick her up and bring her to the W Hotel in Times Square where I was staying. We had a great time and I was a perfect gentleman. We then flew to Florida and stayed at my two-bedroom condo where I continued to be a perfect gentleman. The most I did was hold her hand and pull her through a tight crowd in a nightclub. We had some great discussions on the balcony of my condo. When it was time for her to go back home, I gave her a big hug and said I'd see her soon.

Three weeks later, I had a business meeting in Los Angeles. I called Gia, of course, and she agreed to go out. She invited me to meet her at her workplace, which I thought was a good sign. We went to dinner at a very nice hotel restaurant in Beverly Hills not far from where she worked. We were sitting in the bar, having a couple of drinks before dinner when she looked at me and said, "So what is this? Are you interested in me or what?" I said, "Hell, yeah. That's why I'm here." She smiled and sipped her drink. We flirted all through dinner and the chemistry between us grew more intense by the minute. After dinner, we took a taxi back to my very swanky hotel. We danced for a while in the lounge, then sat down in a little private area. A moment later, I worked up the nerve to lean in for our first kiss. I don't ever remember getting lost in a kiss like that before. It felt like we were melting into each other and the rest of the world had dropped away. At one point, she looked at me and—I'll never forget this—said, "And he kisses good too." That night, we

couldn't stop holding hands and hugging and kiss-
ing each other. From that point on we were dating.
Every two weeks, I'd fly to see her or she'd fly to see
me. We fit in a bunch of great vacations too. I started
thinking about moving to L.A., primarily so I could
have Gia in my arms every day. There was just one
thought in the back of my mind: *This is the one.*

After fourteen months of dating, I felt it was
time to move the relationship forward and also lay
the groundwork for my move to the west coast. Gia
was in terrible financial shape, so she was staying
with family far from her workplace and spending
three hours a day commuting by bus. I wanted to see
her more often and also free up her time to devote to
an entertainment website we had started together
so I signed a one-year lease for a pricey two-bedroom apartment in L.A.

Big mistake. We weren't married. We weren't
even engaged. That was me being presumptuous, me
hoping, wishing, dreaming, and wanting to move
things to a place she might not have been ready for.
Still, I never would have believed that on my birthday sixteen days later, after an argument that ended
with me walking home three miles from a date,
grabbing my suitcase, and leaving for a hotel, that
I'd never spend another night with her. I thought
giving us some breathing room in the heat of the
moment had been the right move; we could then
discuss things in the morning after cooling down.
What I hadn't taken into account was her aban-
donment issues. I should have crashed in our spare
bedroom. The next morning, when I returned to

the apartment, Gia had cooled down so much that I needed a parka as soon as I walked in. She had zero interest in having me around, much less revisiting the events of the previous night. Not being a big fan of the silent treatment, I hopped in a taxi with my suitcases and, as I later heard from her, "abandoned" her again by flying back to Minnesota.

At first, I didn't realize that our romance was dead in the water. Gia and I still talked and texted several times a day, and she often told me how much she missed me. It seemed like nothing had changed, and yet everything had changed. Three months later, after a series of cryptic comments from Gia, it dawned on me that she had no intention of resuming our relationship. I was distraught but didn't see the break as permanent; I remained optimistic that we'd eventually make up.

Here's where I made more mistakes than I could count. I was on the hook not only for her rent, I had also furnished the entire apartment. Plus, I was paying her phone bill, cable bill, Internet bill, car insurance, and even her groceries. I had even bought her a car. I had also invested heavily in equipment and consulting fees to help her start a business venture. I could live with paying her rent; when I make a commitment, I keep my word. That said, I signed the lease hoping that living together part-time would take us to the next level, and eventually marriage. Again, wishful thinking on my part. In hindsight, I should have told her to find housing elsewhere and either used the apartment myself or sublet it. Instead, month after month, I kept shelling out for

Gia's every need. Why? That's easy. I was still in love with her . . . and . . . I . . . just . . . couldn't . . . let . . . go.

Was Gia taking advantage of me? Of course, but only passively. She kept sending me her bills only because I kept paying them.

I see now that throwing money at the relationship was the only concrete way I could cope with my grief about our romance ending. Keeping us financially connected allowed me to actively keep her in my life and hold on to my fantasy of happily ever after.

Then one day after writing yet another rent check, it hit me. Here I thought I was being a knight in shining armor, rescuing a damsel in distress. Instead, by swooping in and saving the day, I had created the classic "enabler/codependent" relationship. I wanted my princess to feel no pain because I loved her so much. But what I actually rescued her from was the responsibility of being accountable for her actions and doing the hard work of making things right.

By trying to protect Gia from the consequences of her actions, I was doing her a disservice. If someone had given me an easy way out from all the adversities I had experienced, I wouldn't have learned vital life lessons and developed the strength, wisdom, and independence I rely on so heavily today. By depriving Gia of opportunities to solve her own problems and cultivate her inner resources, I not only did her more harm than good, I torpedoed any chance we had of ever getting back together.

As soon as I tried to look at the situation through Gia's eyes, I realized the damage I had done. She had taken my financial help because she was out of control and needed it desperately. But consciously or not, she probably didn't feel good about herself for taking advantage of me like that, and that self-recrimination couldn't help but seep into every crevice of our relationship and affect how she interacted with me.

If this had been a healthy, committed relationship in which we were full partners who pooled our resources, my financial help could have strengthened our bond. Instead, it drove a wedge between us. Gia will now look at me as someone who did far more for her than she can ever pay back. Even though I told her that she's free and clear and doesn't owe me a penny, that debt will always be hanging in the air between us; and every time we see or talk to each other will be one more reminder of the mess she had gotten herself into. If our positions were reversed, I know I'd have a hard time feeling relaxed and open around someone I felt I owed so much to. In fact, I'd be so uncomfortable around that person, I'd want to keep my distance, both physically and emotionally.

Once I had that epiphany, I took immediate steps to stop the bleeding and salvage whatever I could of the relationship. I sent her this e-mail:

Gia, I haven't given up on being together with you again someday. But if this is what you truly want, just to be friends, then I have to restructure this relationship in my mind and treat you as I do my other friends. If they need help, I do help them, but not to this extent. Giving you so much is unfair to my family and to the other people who need my help. It's also unfair to my future partner because

I'm spending money that could be our money. I'm also investing emotional energy and time in you that could be spent finding my true life partner. It's not your fault that you don't love me the way that I love you. But it's not my responsibility to support you.

It felt good to clear the air like that, but I couldn't figure out why I was feeling a sense of déjà vu. Then epiphany number two struck me like a thunderbolt: I had made the same mistake with Liliana fifteen years earlier. In both cases, I fell madly in love with a woman and everything started out great; then I realized she had some serious issues to deal with and could use my help. In both cases, I unintentionally sabotaged the relationship by trying to solve those issues for them in whatever way I could. It wasn't like I was trying to buy the affection of these women. I just have a hero complex; and frankly, that's a part of me I'm still not willing to part with just yet.

Even though Liliana and I were actually living together and planning to be married, footing the entire bill for her and her kids proved to be our undoing. Years later, Liliana told me that therapy had helped her to understand why she had had an affair: She had felt I was so much of a prince that she wasn't worthy of me. Wow. I had no idea. If I had it to do over again, I would have suggested pooling our money together so we'd each have a sense of ownership of our combined resources. Liliana would have then felt like a valued partner instead of just a receiver.

You'd think that my experience with Liliana would have crossed my mind as I was writing check after check for Gia. Nope, not for a second. Love clouded my judgment and I saw only what I wanted to see. I was so happy that I was taking financial pressures off of Gia that I didn't realize I was putting a different kind of pressure on her. Yes, her financial stress was relieved but I inadvertently and irrevocably changed the dynamics of how we related to each other. It's no surprise then that I ended up tucked away in a safe little corner in Gia's life, which is the last place I wanted to be.

I find it especially puzzling that I reverted back to my Liliana-era mindset considering that in between my relationships with Liliana and Gia, I was involved with Krissy for eight years. Krissy had been a paragon of financial virtue. She made less money than what Gia was making, yet she had money in the bank and had paid off her car well ahead of the loan repayment time period. Krissy was not only self-sufficient, she insisted on paying half of our expenses, even during vacations.

Krissy and I started dating in the early days of Advanced Lighting. The company was poised to take off but my credit was poor due to the debt I had rung up while working for FiberNev and TexGlow. I was operating Advanced Lighting by juggling my credit cards, debit card, and cash flow because I didn't have a single credit card with a high enough limit to fly to a trade show, book a hotel room, and rent a car. It was a big headache because I had to travel a lot.

One day, Krissy said, "Listen, why don't I add you as a user to my credit card and you can just pay the bill every month?" That floored me. It was the first time a woman had ever offered to do something like that for me. Still, I told her, "No, I couldn't do that. I need your help but I'd feel responsible if something bad happened." But Krissy insisted and finally convinced me. Every month, I paid employees first, then employee taxes and our facility rent, and then I paid Krissy's credit card.

Eight years later when I sold Advanced Lighting, my relationship with Krissy had been over for about a year. As a thank you for everything she did to help and support me and the business, I sent her a check for $10,000. She did *not* want to accept it. She said, "I didn't do anything, Paul. I just let you use my card." I said, "No, you did a lot. You put yourself in a vulnerable position. I don't know if I would have been who I am without your help."

In my view, the way Krissy and I handled finances was the responsible way to give and receive help. That said, I never thought any less of Liliana or Gia for having financial problems. How could I? I had been in worse shape myself. I remember telling Gia, "Hey, I've been there. I'm not judging you, I'm just trying to help. Let's focus on the solution to the problem, not on what got you there." Of course, I also worked with her to address the patterns of thinking and behavior that got her into trouble in the first place.

I see now that funneling so much money to Gia after we had stopped dating was a huge mistake, but it's not the money itself I have regrets about. I can hold my head up high about that because I was coming from a good place and trying to help out the woman I loved and cared for. Yes, I was initially motivated to help her because I thought we had a future together. But even more than that I wanted her to succeed; I wanted her to blossom and be everything she could be. She is now in better control of her life, which I'm very happy about. What I feel terrible about is that I unwittingly undermined a relationship that meant the world to me.

Ultimately, I have no one to blame but myself for the way things unraveled. I should have recognized what was happening based on my experience with Liliana. Sure, I wish Gia would have stepped up and said, "Paul, I'm interested in seeing other people. I don't see you as my life partner so it's not right to continue this arrangement. I need the financial help but I can't accept it because I know that it's coming from a place of love for me and I can't give you that same love back." Then again, even if she had looked me in the eye and said those words, I probably would have protested. I was as desperate to win her back as she was for my financial assistance. In the end, we both got what we needed at the time. Unfortunately, we both paid an awfully steep price for it.

The good news is I'm wiser and more aware than I was before I had met Gia, and am now better equipped to be in a healthy relationship. I understand now that I have no right to judge Gia in any way; all I can do is take ownership of my own part in the deterioration of our relationship. Being with Gia had been a great gift in my life, and my newfound awareness was one more gift I could thank her for. Giving me her love, as well as taking it away, has made me a better man.

Love And Money
Your Life, Your Thoughts

- How do you view people who are genuinely positive and upbeat, especially in the face of challenging circumstances?

- When you're happy and positive instead of cynical and pessimistic, how do people respond to you differently?

- In what ways can you change your thinking in order to move toward a more positive attitude?

- What are the advantages of patiently allowing a potential relationship to unfold naturally rather than forcing intimacy at the first opportunity?

- What are the dangers in making financial commitments to someone you love but are not yet officially committed to?

- How can you learn coping strategies that will help you keep your temper in check during an argument so that you avoid saying and doing things you will later regret?

- Looking back at how your previous relationships ended, what could you have done differently to help you move through your grief or anger more quickly and in a healthier manner?

- In what ways did you contribute to the end of a previous relationship that you refused to take responsibility for at the time?

- When you "rescue" another person from their self-created problems, in what ways may you actually be doing them a disservice?

- In what ways, if any, are dependency issues compromising the integrity of your romantic relationship?

- What needs to be said to your partner that you haven't yet found the courage to say?

- How do concerns left unspoken affect the dynamics of your relationship?

- What do you fear may happen if you compassionately and respectfully confront the issues in your relationship?

- What are three things you can do right now that will make your partner feel more valued and cared for?

- What negative patterns, if any, from your previous relationships have manifested in your current relationship?

- When your love for another is tainted by insecurity, idealistic thinking, or desperation, how can you shift your mindset to view your current circumstances as an opportunity for personal growth that will ultimately solidify and deepen your relationship?

DARING TO BE CARING

In 1987 I was sharing an apartment with two other flight attendants, both of them women. I was twenty-four, carefree, and living for the moment. In other words, I was clueless and irresponsible. I spent all my money going out, having fun, and buying stuff I didn't really need. As a result, I'd run out of money for gas and was always one paycheck behind in my rent. I was never quite ready for a bill I knew was coming.

Damina, one of my roommates, was in charge of collecting our share of the rent and writing out the check to the landlord. One day she finally got sick of my excuses and said in a caring way, "You've gotta get your act together, Paul. You need to be more responsible. You're a grown man. You can't live like this forever." Ouch. A guy never wants to hear that he's immature, especially from a pretty girl. Of course, I proved her point by snapping back and deflecting the issue. "Oh, yeah?" I brilliantly countered before stomping off. "Well, you were born with a silver spoon in your mouth. You have a rich dad and never had to worry about money like I have." I was glad that Damina was leaving on a flight the next day and wouldn't be home for a week. Just the thought of seeing her ticked me off.

A couple of days later I was sitting home alone on the couch, still stewing about how mean Damina had been to me. But by that time, my excuses were starting to ring a bit hollow and my tendency for introspection managed to kick in. In a flash, I realized that I was focusing all my energy on how much Damina's comment hurt me and none whatsoever to whether there was any truth to it. Immediately chastened, I saw that my indignation was a smoke-screen for my desire to continue treating life like one big party. I had two choices in that interaction: get honest or get angry, and I had taken the easy way out. For the sake of my self-respect, I knew I had to be brutally honest with myself and think hard about the message behind Damina's scolding.

The first conclusion I came to was that Damina was walking her talk by living responsibly. She had a great work ethic, never missed rent or a car payment, and always seemed to have enough left over to buy nice clothes and do fun things with her friends. When I looked at how I handled my own money, I had to admit that Damina was right. It wasn't an issue of me not having enough money, it was an issue of me being completely undisciplined. I thought, *What kind of a man am I? How am I going* to keep a girlfriend if I can't afford things I should be able to afford? Right then and there, I decided to get my priorities in order. First, I was going to think twice before spending any money. Next, I would bring in more money by picking up more flights. Working more would also mean I'd have less opportunities to waste money drinking and partying. By the time I got up off that couch, I was a changed man.

Fifteen years later, I was able to tell Damina what a profound effect her words had on me, and I thanked her for having the guts to put our friendship at risk by telling me what I needed to hear. Sometimes I find myself wondering, if not for Damina, how many more years would I have wasted acting like a frat boy before I finally wised up? Would any of my other friends have stepped up and word-slapped some sense into me? Isn't that what good friends are supposed to do—challenge and encourage each other to shape up even when it's uncomfortable to do so?

A few years after Damina's impromptu intervention, I had the opportunity to return the favor by compassionately confronting Ken, my best friend at American Airlines, about a sensitive issue in his life. Ken and I had met at the Charm Farm, the campus in Dallas-Fort Worth where the airline trained its pilots and flight attendants. Ken was a young, handsome, good ol' Southern boy who got a lot of attention from girls but was clueless about how to interact with them. Fortunately, thanks to my expert tutelage, he caught on quickly.

As flight attendants, we had a lot of time off. We'd meet at my apartment complex, sit by the pool, and make our way through a case of beer. A bunch of other flight attendants lived at the same complex and we'd all play volleyball and have a lot of fun together. In those days, we all did a lot of social drinking, but Ken took it further than the rest of us. He'd never get stupid drunk, but I started noticing that he always had a beer or a Jim Beam and Coke in his hand. He even had a special glass that he carried with him everywhere he went—emphasis on *everywhere*. I was reluctant to say anything because I didn't see any evidence that his drinking was having a negative effect; he did a great job at work and always acted responsibly.

I was so happy for Ken when he met Carly. They were a perfect match. They eventually decided to get married and move to Nashville so he could be closer to his family in Alabama. Ken and I stayed in close contact; in fact, we talked just about every other day. So I was eager to see him a year later when he flew back to Dallas for a visit. I was on my way to pick him up at the airport when my phone rang. It was Carly, and I could instantly hear the concern in her voice. She said, "Paul, I wanted to talk to you before you pick Ken up. I'm really worried about him. He's constantly drinking. I don't know what to say or how to say it. We're going to have a baby soon and I just don't what to do." I said, "I'm glad you let me know, Carly. I won't tell Ken you said anything; I'll just figure out a way to bring it up."

Ken stayed with me a couple of days and we had a great time. I did notice that Carly was right about his drinking; if anything, it had gotten worse.

On the drive back to the airport, I said, "Ken, I just want you to know you mean a lot to me and I'm really glad you could come for a visit. It was great hanging out with you again. I've got something I want to say that I think is so important that I'm willing to put our friendship on the line. How you react is up to you but I want you to know that I love you and I'm coming from a good place." I could already tell that Ken was withdrawing and getting defensive, but I was expecting that. I said, "I noticed that you're drinking as much as ever, if not more, and that concerns me, especially because you've got a wife and family depending on you and they need you at your best. We're older now and have more responsibilities and I hope you can taper off your drinking before it becomes a problem. If I can help, just say the word and I'll do what I can."

Ken did not take it well. Just like I had reacted to Damina, he was angry and offended and just sat there steaming until we got to the airport. Without a word, he grabbed his suitcase and disappeared into the terminal. I was okay with that because I couldn't have lived with myself if I had chickened out and his drinking later caused some real damage. I didn't hear from Ken again until nearly a year later, and then we just picked up as if nothing had happened. The conversation was never mentioned again, although I continued to hear reports from our mutual friends that they routinely smelled alcohol on him when he was flying.

Eight years after his visit, my phone rang after midnight. It was Ken, calling from a Washington D.C.

hotel. He was crying uncontrollably and confessed he had just been fired. He said the airline apparently had someone watching him and that they tested him for alcohol at the end of the flight that evening. "I don't know how I'm going to tell Carly," he said between sobs. "I'm a failure. I failed her and my kids." I tried to comfort him but he was too distraught. He said, "I keep going back to what you told me years ago, Paul. You thought I was drinking too much and I got upset with you. But you were right. I wish I would've listened to you; I *should've* listened to you."

I finally said, "You know what, Ken? Lots of people have had this problem; it's how you react to it that's going to set you apart from everybody else. There's no need to wake up Carly and get her all upset. You're better off telling her face to face. Just go home tomorrow, sit her down, and tell her the truth. Tell her exactly how you feel and how you plan on getting help and fixing this. Maybe you don't have an answer yet, but you'll find it once you start looking. Chances are, Carly's going to understand because she already knows about your drinking and in a weird way, she might even be relieved because you finally hit bottom and now you're ready to take ownership of it. Listen, Ken, you're a good man. This is just a hiccup; you can fix this and have a great life with your family."

The next day when Ken got home, he told Carly everything. She was extremely upset but very understanding and supportive. That Sunday they went to church, and Ken told his story in front of the entire congregation. He was embarrassed and scared but he dealt with it like an adult and didn't hold anything back. Everyone in his church embraced him and supported him as he got sober, attended AA meetings, and started working his way back. Someone in the church even found him a new job so he could provide for his family.

I couldn't have been prouder of Ken as he rebuilt his life. By the time I saw him again, he was in amazing shape and I told him how jealous I was. He said, "Oh, man, Paul, I'm working out every day. I never knew I could feel so good!" I was especially happy for him when the flight attendant's union called him two years after his firing to tell him he was getting his job back. The union's contract required the airline to offer treatment to any employees who were struggling with alcoholism, and the new guidelines were retroactive. Ken had to agree to more frequent urine tests, but since he was clean and sober that wasn't a problem.

I'm thrilled that Ken made it all the way back and is now living the life he was meant to live. He's in great physical shape, has a stronger marriage, and is a better role model for his children. Looking back, I think the concern I expressed to Ken on the way to the airport in some small way helped prepare him for the battle ahead. I know that my speaking up out of love and concern ended up deepening the bond between us, even though it angered him at the time. Ultimately, the way I see it, friendships worth having are friendships worth risking.

Daring To Be Caring
Your Life, Your Thoughts

- What incidents can you recall in which a friend of yours took the risk of telling you something they thought you needed to hear?

- How has your reaction to constructive criticism evolved over the years?

- If you get defensive or angry when hearing constructive criticism, what do you think is stopping you from listening to it and asking yourself if any of it might be true?

- How can you get better at accepting constructive criticism without getting defensive or angry?

- If you took a long, hard look in the mirror, what do you think you'd see about yourself that could stand improvement?

- Who in your life needs a dose of tough love and what's stopping you from giving it to them?

- How does not speaking up about an important personal issue affect your relationship with that person?

- Why is offering constructive criticism to someone you care about good for both of you?

Closing Thoughts

I wrote this book to deliver a powerful message. So I hope you close these pages with one thought in mind: *I can overcome anything and live a life without limits.* Because you can.

Hey, if I can do it, you can too. My challenges were childhood abuse, years of Special Ed, getting ripped off by unethical bosses, two battles with cancer, disappointing relationships, and every kind of business problem I could imagine and then some. But I'm here today, happy, healthy, wealthy, and excited about life.

My story is your story. Sure, the details may differ but you know my hopes and heartaches as well as you know your own. I also want you to know this: Adversity is the gateway to greatness, and life will present you only with obstacles you are capable of overcoming.

The richer, more fulfilling life you can only imagine today is waiting for you on the other side of tomorrow. How do you get there? Through ferocious self-honesty, a commitment to lifelong learning, an uncompromising work ethic, and assuming full responsibility for every one of your thoughts, words, and actions.

Don't wait another day to start moving toward your very best self. My story is proof that you can balance outer success with inner peace and be happier than you ever thought possible. Believe in yourself, believe in your dreams, and you will be unstoppable.

About The Author

As founder and CEO of Minnesota-based Advanced Lighting Systems, Inc., a manufacturer of LED and fiber optics used in entertainment and architectural lighting, Paul Streitz established himself as an industry visionary and the go-to-source for high-tech, high-touch creative lighting solutions for everything from the Grammy awards, Broadway shows, and major concert tours to unprecedented billboard events for Times Square. Advanced Lighting also provided the technical know-how and lighting products to illuminate the original Declaration of Independence and all its supporting documents at the National Archives in Washington D.C.

Paul's extraordinary journey took him from working-class roots to founder of a nationally respected lighting company to author and motivational speaker. Along the way, he overcame debilitating childhood insecurities, shocking betrayals at work and at home, and two life-changing bouts with cancer. Ultimately, with integrity, ingenuity, and indomitable will, he created a rich, fulfilling life and a business worth millions.

Learn more at **PaulStreitz.com**

Follow Paul on Twitter at **twitter.com/paulstreitz**

Find Paul on Facebook at
facebook.com/PaulStreitzFanpage
facebook.com/BlueCollarBuddha

Notes

Notes

Notes

Notes

Made in the USA
Lexington, KY
14 January 2012